100

OF THE WORLD'S TALLEST BUILDINGS

Thomas Schaller, Schaller Architectural Illustration
courtesy Otis Elevator Co.

100
OF THE
WORLD'S
TALLEST
BUILDINGS

Council on Tall Buildings and Urban Habitat

Ivan Zaknic
Matthew Smith
Dolores Rice

Gingko
PRESS

This edition published in 1998 by
Gingko Press Inc.
5768 Paradise Drive, Suite J
Corte Madera, CA, 94925, USA
Telephone:+(415) 924 9615 Facsimile:+(415) 924 9608
E-mail: gingko@linex.com

First published in Australia in 1998 by
The Images Publishing Group Pty Ltd
ACN 059 734 431

ISBN 3 927258 60 1

Primary Research by Ivan Zaknic
Text by Ivan Zaknic and Matt Smith with editing by Dolores Rice
Illustrations compiled by Ivan Zaknic and Dolores Rice
Editor-in-Chief: Lynn S. Beedle

Designed by the Graphic Image Studio, Australia

Printed in Hong Kong

Contents

Preface

The publication of *100 of the World's Tallest Buildings* is the culmination of a project that has been years in the making. From its very conception by the late Jerry Iffland, a structural engineer whose interest in tall buildings belied his actual practice in building bridges, to the thousands of hours of research, writing, editing, phone calls, and correspondence worldwide, it has been an experience that has taught us much not only about the wondrous structures that grace our cities around the world, but also about the generosity of time and spirit of the people that have helped us in this journey.

The initial idea was to prepare a book entitled *The 100 Tallest Buildings of the World*. As work continued, however, we quickly came to realize that the list of the 100 tallest was in a state of constant flux. Almost monthly, we were receiving new information—not only about buildings that were just breaking ground, but also about buildings that had already been in existence but went unreported for one reason or another. An example of this were the tall buildings that came to the fore with the opening of the former USSR to the world. But information on these buildings is still difficult to come by.

Thus was born *100 of the World's Tallest Buildings*, in which the tall building professionals have produced a wonderful collection of the tallest and most fascinating high-rises that have been constructed around the globe. Their existence spans more than 65 years of engineering and architectural excellence—from the 1930s splendor of the Chrysler Building and the Empire State Building, to the magnificence of the Petronas Towers, still under construction and due to be completed in 1998. The buildings themselves span in height from 725 feet to more than double at 1,483 feet tall. We added a section on tall buildings under construction, recognizing that many of the world's most magnificent towers will be those that are not yet completed.

Skyscrapers represent man's very nature to continue to reach ever higher toward the heavens, creating lasting monuments to their own ingenuity and courage. This publication presents 100 of these very special skyscrapers. We hope you will enjoy their beauty, majesty, and individuality.

Council on Tall Buildings and Urban Habitat
Dolores Rice
Lynn S. Beedle

Introduction

"What can the experiences of the past tell those who will design even taller skyscrapers in the new millennium?"

We put that question to architect John Portman of John Portman and Associates, Inc., and structural engineer Duncan Michael of Ove Arup & Partners, each intimately involved with some of the most recognized tall buildings around the world. —Ed.

High-Rise Design

High-rise structures in the future hold great potential for making our urban centers better places to live. The single-purpose towers that have placed landmark signatures on the skylines of most of the world's major cities are now being re-examined. The multi-use tower is now taking on increased scrutiny as a response to the growing need for a more responsive urban architecture.

By combining multiple functions such as office, hotel, apartments, and retail within a single high-rise tower, we are now applying the 'coordinate unit' principle to a single structure. For years I have based our urban planning on the ideal of creating 'coordinate units' wherein all the basic needs of an individual are provided with a radius which is no larger than the distance one is willing to walk without using vehicular transportation. In America that distance is usually 7–10 minutes. The popularity of mixed-use development grew from the fact that this concept is convenient and practical.

In the future we see great advantage in high-rise developments that create a coordinate unit within one tower while recognizing human scale and open space at its base. Single buildings in which one can work, live, shop, and play will create a new urban lifestyle, relying on wheels less and less.

In the post-war years after World War II, the increased use of the automobile radically changed our cities' development. There was a vast horizontal sprawl as the suburbs grew rapidly away from the city. With more cars travelling longer distances came traffic congestion, inconvenience, and air pollution, while fragmenting the city socially and physically.

Today our goal is to reduce the use of automobiles, creating less fragmentation while providing a more pedestrian-friendly lifestyle. Making our cities more vertical by creation of multi-use high-rise projects will improve our air quality and decrease the amount of time we need to go from Point A to Point B. Pedestrian activity will be at a smaller scale within our urban centers. Environment problems will be reduced and a new urban lifestyle will improve the quality of life in our cities. This, of course, will only work in the context of broad planning of the built space to open space with pedestrian scale, use, and nature taken into consideration.

John Portman
John Portman and Associates, Inc.
Atlanta, Georgia, USA

A Recent Achievement

Very tall buildings are a recent achievement of man, about the same age as the electron in our paradigm. One can demonstrate a historic lineage of lighthouses, pagodas and church spires, but the nature of such a reference base confirms the newness of the existence of very tall inhabited buildings. Our achievements to date are still raw and often naive. It is wonderful to be young and we need not apologize for the limited progress made to date.

Tall buildings generate a reaction in every citizen. One is either for them or against them, but one cannot ignore or deny them. They get invented in moments of optimism which can easily transform into ambition and even statements of power or arrival. Whether tall buildings get still taller or not matters little. Compared to the human, 200, 400, 600, or 800 meters are all much the same. Compared to another tall building one meter may, of course, matter a lot.

Technology will march on and new configurations, combinations and materials will each get their chance. Will structure and enclosure coalesce again as in traditional construction, taking one whole component out of the time and cost game? The ideas within the term intelligent building will develop and find great favor. If energy ever does get expensive, the intelligent facade will have its place and would affect the facade cum structure issue crucially. Access to and within the big volume will change, partly by better mobility, partly by information technology, and partly by much more visibility.

It is doubtful if profit will ever be the driving force for very tall buildings. If you just want to get rich, there are better ways to do it. The other imagination gripping construction of our time is the big bridge. Unlike the tall building which has only one end, the bridge knows exactly where it is going. The quest for longer spans is the equivalent of the quest for taller buildings.

In about 100 years from now, the tall building will be expected to take its proper place in our cities and no longer be the defiant teenager of the urban family. As we expand our virtual worlds we will need still more the comfort and certainty of the demonstrably fixed and tangible.

Duncan Michael
Ove Arup Partnership
London, England

100 of the World's Tallest Buildings

Billed as the spearhead for the rejuvenation of Detroit's downtown, Renaissance Center is much more than a mixed use complex on the waterfront. It is the city's Eiffel Tower, the symbol of the rebirth of Detroit. Completed in 1981, the project occupies 33 acres and is used by an estimated 20,000 people daily. The complex includes the 73-story Renaissance One hotel in the center, surrounded by four 39-story office towers, which surmount a three-story retail podium. Two 21-story office towers and two earthen berms which house mechanical units are also a part of the complex.

The cylindrical tower is 128 feet in diameter. The base of the tower contains an 88-foot-high lobby arranged around concrete columns, which rise from the foundation caissons to the elevator core of the tower. The rooms of the hotel are enclosed by a concrete honeycomb-like structure, which is sufficiently stiff to significantly diminish the wind drift of the tower compared to other buildings its size.

Atop the tower are three levels of restaurants reached by two elevators in a 24-foot-diameter external tower attached to the side of the building. Encircling the hotel are street-level meeting rooms sheathed in reinforced concrete, linked to the lobby of the tower by a skylighted enclosed walkway. The complex features computer-controlled environmental, safety, and security systems.

Before renovation, the 16 identical entrances to the hotel, the retail area, and the four office towers, made orientation within the Renaissance Center podium area confusing. The hotel registration desk was situated in the heart of the circulation pattern, which crossed office workers and shoppers with users of the hotel. Renovations increased signage throughout the podium, placed a marque above the hotel entrance, organized the retail stores on the first level on one wing, and delineated different spaces with distinct materials. The expansive lobby was partitioned with increased plantings and new materials, which served to diminish the overpowering effect of the columns. These improvements have served to revitalize the complex and create the thriving image that the city of Detroit was seeking.

Renaissance One

Location: Detroit, Michigan, USA
Completion: 1977
Height: 725ft (221m)
Stories: 73
Area: 1.4 million ft²
Structure: Concrete
Cladding: Reflective glass and concrete
Use: Hotel

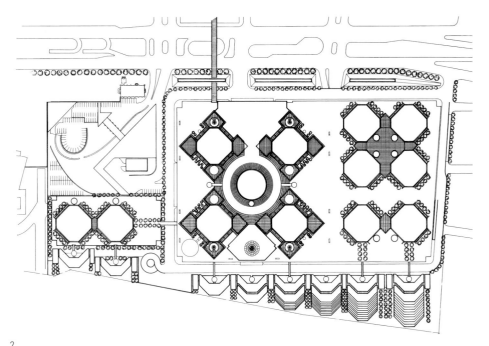

2

1 Renaissance One is a shimmering tower of glass reaching
   for the sky (Opposite)
2 Site plan
3 Renaissance Center, with Renaissance One towering high
4 Renaissance Center glimmers in the Detriot skyline
Photography: Michael Portman courtesy John Portman
& Associates (1,3,4)

3

4

Architect: John Portman & Associates, Inc.
Structural Engineer: John Portman & Associates, Inc.
Mechanical Engineer: Britt Alderman Associates
Electrical Engineer: Morris Harrison & Associates
Developer: Ford Land Development Company
Contractor: Tishman Construction Co.

With the dawn of the steel frame and the elevator came a basic shift in building construction. Where once the exterior shells of buildings served both structural and environmental purposes, steel allowed the development of the structure as purely load-bearing, while an applied skin was attached to the structure to shelter the building from the elements. Nowhere is this more evident than in the construction of tall steel and concrete buildings which receive expensive skins of granite and glass. While some notable buildings have expressed their structure on the exterior, few have integrated their structure into the skin of the building. One Mellon Bank Center has achieved this integration by combining a steel tube structure with panels of steel on the exterior skin to form a rigid structure which supports building load while resisting wind sway.

Typically a steel tube structure connects closely spaced columns along the exterior with columns around the interior service cores to create two tubes which act together to support the loads of the building while resisting wind forces. In One Mellon Bank Center, the arrangement of the small core necessitated the elimination of stiffer members and diagonal bracing. For a tube system to work, the columns in the core and the exterior need to be connected by a beam in a straight line, but the columns in the core of One Mellon Bank Center are connected at angles. While this arrangement of columns and beams supports the load as mandated by codes, they do not control the sway of the building as caused by wind. The addition of the steel exterior skin created a unified tube strong enough to bring the sway into comfortable limits.

Window glass was inserted into the steel panel openings using neoprene gaskets similar to the windows in an airplane fuselage. Minimizing the glass area to a quarter of each panel helped conserve energy and maintain the structural integrity of each panel, while giving the building a visual weight similar to other historic buildings in the area. Extensive analysis determined where to reinforce each panel, while a full-scale mock-up, tested at Lehigh University in Bethlehem, Pennsylvania, proved the analyses to be accurate. During erection each panel was attached to the columns at the center of the panel and to the panels on the sides. This allowed the columns to shorten from the weight of the floors above before the panels were secured, to ensure that the panels would not buckle. Each panel was painted a warm gray to complement the granite of the nearby Allegheny County Courthouse and contrast the rich brown of the USX Tower across the street.

The tower's elongated octagonal plan serves to diminish the apparent width of the building. An attached 17-story bustle, with its mansard style top, reminiscent of the nearby Union Trust Building, matches the courthouse height. At the corners, projections create eight corner offices with bay windows.

One Mellon Bank Center

Location: Pittsburgh, Pennsylvania, USA
Completion: 1984
Height: 727ft (221.6m)
Stories: 54
Area: 1.7 million ft²
Structure: Steel
Cladding: Steel plate face panels
Use: Office

3

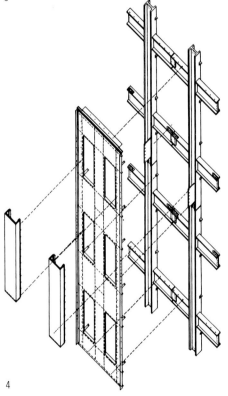

4

1 View of tower (Opposite)
2 Tower takes on hue of setting sun
3 Pedestrian's view
4 Stressed skin-tube interface
Photography: Boyd courtesy Ellerbe Becket Company (1,2);
Associated Photographers Inc. courtesy Ellerbe Becket (3)

Architect: Welton Beckett Associates
Structural Engineer: Lev Zetlin Associates
Services Engineer: Lehr Associates
Developer: U.S.Steel Realty Development
General Contractor: Turner Construction Company

Olympia Centre is a major multi-use addition to Chicago's Magnificent Mile. The 728-foot 63-story building includes over 200 luxury condominiums, 327,000 square feet of office space, a four-story retail store, and a three-and one-half-level basement parking garage.

The building's massing combines low-rise and high-rise portions. This solution preserves the low- to mid-rise character of Michigan Avenue and Superior Street while reinforcing the open-space edge along Chicago Avenue, thus providing better views for the condominiums in the upper half of the tower and allowing the department store more freedom in structure and layout.

The tower combines a reinforced concrete exterior tube with conventionally reinforced concrete flat-slab floors in the condominiums and a joist-slab floor system in the office, department store, and parking garage portions. The low-rise structure is framed in steel above grade and concrete below.

The entire exterior of the building is clad in Swedish pink granite of varying finishes. The windows are glazed with tinted and insulated glass in coated aluminum frames.

A Neiman Marcus department store occupies most of the grade level and all of levels two, three, and four, containing approximately 198,000 square feet of store area. Vertical transportation within the store is provided by pairs of escalators within a skylight atrium in the south portion and two elevators within the tower. The major store entrance, located on Michigan Avenue, features a two-story arch in which glass substitutes for the traditional keystone.

The 430-car self-park garage can be accessed by three shuttle elevators; one for condominium residents and two for the office tenants and department store users.

Condominiums comprise the top 39 floors of the tower. Level 24 is the club level, providing amenities including a lounge, party rooms and catering kitchen, swimming pool, lockers, exercise room, and racquetball court.

The model apartment at Olympia Centre was designed for a hypothetical, childless, professional couple who like to entertain. The two-bedroom apartment contains 1,800 square feet, whose second bedroom can be converted into a den or study, its divider wall replaced with pocket doors.

Levels 58 through 63 accommodate six levels of special penthouse condominiums incorporating duplex spaces, exterior terraces and balconies. The condominiums are served by four elevators rising directly from the lobby on Chicago Avenue, giving a significantly different quality to the low-rise and high-rise components.

Olympia Centre

Location: Chicago, Illinois, USA
Completion: 1986
Height: 728ft (221.9m)
Stories: 63
Area: 1.42 million ft²
Structure: Mixed
**Cladding: Granite, tinted & insulated glass, coated
    aluminium frames**
Use: Multiple

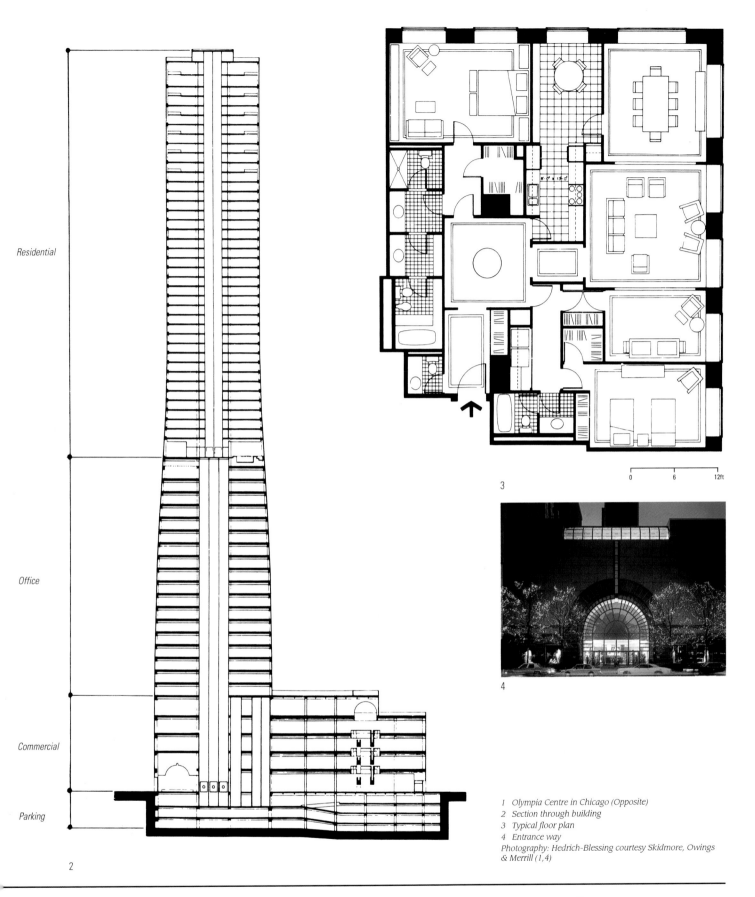

Residential

Office

Commercial

Parking

2

3

4

1 Olympia Centre in Chicago (Opposite)
2 Section through building
3 Typical floor plan
4 Entrance way
Photography: Hedrich-Blessing courtesy Skidmore, Owings
& Merrill (1,4)

0   6   12ft

Architect: Skidmore, Owings & Merrill (SOM)
Structural Engineer: SOM
Services Engineer: SOM with Jaros, Baum & Bolles
Developers: Chicago Superior and Associates,
    Olympia & York/LMI, Equity Financial and
    Management Company

The Carlton Centre multi-use complex, completed in 1972, was at that time the largest commercial development in Africa and the first major redevelopment in downtown Johannesburg. It has since served as a catalyst for other developments in the area. Four small blocks, characteristic of a city dating back to the time when it was little more than a miner's camp, were incorporated into one 'superblock.' Parts of two other blocks were also developed concurrently.

The complex consists of a 50-story office tower, a 624-room hotel, and two below-grade concourse levels. In addition, the project includes two major department stores, exhibition space, and parking in two facilities. Two buildings stand out above ground: the 30-story Carlton Hotel with its bell-bottom base, and the 50-story Carlton Centre Tower soaring above, with its tremendous jump in scale for the city. The main architectural elements of the complex are grouped around a large circular court which penetrates the two shopping levels below the plaza.

Much of the street level is open for pedestrians, landscaped areas, and open courts. The landscaped areas also include fountains, sidewalk cafés, and a skating rink, all of which represent a substantial increase in the amount of open public space downtown. Below the plaza the two lower shopping levels are joined to the major shopping concourse. The concourse contains 180 retail shops, restaurants, and banks, providing shoppers with a traffic-free, all-weather shopping complex connected vertically by escalators and elevators to the high-rise buildings as well as to the parking areas. A service level immediately below the shopping concourse is reserved exclusively for the delivery of goods.

The foundations of the two high-rise buildings are 3.5 meters in diameter reinforced concrete caissons that extend to bedrock, 20 meters below the bottom of the main excavation, which itself is 30 meters deep.

The office tower has a 230-meter-high, slip-formed reinforced concrete core and perimeter columns tapering from three square meters at street level to one square meter at the top. Spandrel beams support ribbed slabs at each floor level.

The Carlton Centre Office tower is the tallest building in Africa at 730 feet. All the buildings in the complex have a reinforced concrete structure with an exposed exterior aggregate, and an integral finish of local gray granite exposed by sand-blasting.

1

2

Carlton Centre Tower

Location: Johannnesburg, South Africa
Completion: 1972
Height: 730ft (222.5m)
Stories: 50
Area: 1.1 million ft²
Structure: Concrete
Cladding: Gray granite
Use: Multiple

3

4

6

5

1 Carlton Center Tower stands tall in the Johannesburg
   skyline (Opposite)
2 Bird's eye view of the buildings (Opposite)
3 Circular stairway in shopping concourse
4 Public courtyard
5 Closeup view
6 Elevation
*Photography: Ezra Stoller Esto Photographics courtesy
Skidmore, Owings & Merrill (2,3,4,5,6)*

Architect: Skidmore, Owings & Merrill
Associate Architect: W. Rhodes-Harrison, Hoffe
    & Partners
Structural Engineer: Weidlinger & Associates
    with Ove Arup & Partners
Services Engineer: Syska & Hennessy Inc.
    with Watson, Edwards, Van der Spry & Partners
Developer: Carlton Centre, Ltd
General Contractor: Murray & Roberts

The 732-foot skyscraper simply called 1600 Smith Street is located in the southern portion of the central business district of Houston, Texas. It is in the form of an irregular 'Y' covering 4.4 acres—an area of more than three city blocks. Both the tower and the garage adjacent to it open onto a central plaza, located so as to receive the most predominant pedestrian flow at the corner of Smith and Pease Streets. The landscaped plaza, 4.5 feet above the street level, features a fountain and greenery, and echoes the form of the tower within all its variations. It is paved with warm pink granite. A skywalk across Pease Street connects the building to the Whitehall Hotel, and an underground tunnel links the building to Four Allen Center.

The five-sided tower, 55 stories high, steps back three times at the back (at the 39th, 47th, and 51st floors), whereas the front runs the full height, terminating in an octagonal domed top. There are three entrances at the first floor and one on the second, connecting the tower to the garage. The monumental formal Smith Street entrance, three stories high, leads to the main lobby. The lobby interior is covered in flame-cut Sardinian granite. A grand staircase leads to the concourse level.

The tower exterior is also sheathed in flame-cut Sardinian gray granite, with dark gray windows with double-pane glass set in black frames designed to punctuate the stone facade. As the tower rises, the full-length windows decrease slightly in size to accentuate the building's height while reducing the ratio of glass to masonry and increasing energy efficiency.

Structural steel was chosen over other systems because of its cost efficiency and column sizes. Wind loads are carried by an exterior partial-tube frame with columns at ten-foot intervals. The tube elements are tied together at three locations to minimize deformation due to torsion. The floor framing consists of composite steel beams with two-inch galvanized metal deck and a lightweight concrete floor slab.

1600 Smith Street presents a strong urban image against the Houston skyline, and projects a friendly relationship at the pedestrian level.

1600 Smith Street

Location: Houston, Texas, USA
Completion: 1984
Height: 732ft (223.1m)
Stories: 55
Area: 1.23 million ft²
Structure: Steel
Cladding: Sardinian gray granite
Use: Office

1 1600 Smith Street by day (Opposite)
2 Site Plan
3 Interior view of main entrance lobby facing Smith Street
4 Three-story main entrance
Photography: Paul Hester courtesy Morris Architects (1,3,4)

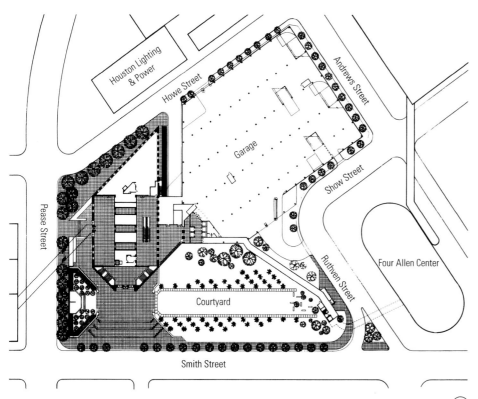

2

3

4

Architect: Morris Architects
Landscape Architect: The SWA Group
Structural Engineer: CBM Engineers, Inc.
Mechanical Engineer: I.A. Naman & Associates, Inc.
Civil Engineer: Walter P. Moore and Associates, Inc.
Developers: Cullen Center, Inc. and PIC Realty
  Corporation

Owner: Cullen Center, Inc. and PIC Realty
  Corporation
General Contractor: Linback Construction

The Washington Mutual Tower is, in a sense, two buildings. One, the base, is designed to interact with the surrounding street grid and the pedestrian/automobile environment around it. The second, the Tower, is a welcome and well-placed addition to the skyline. With cream colored granite and blue-green reflective glass skin, the Tower rests upon the base independent of its immediate surroundings yet in harmony with them. The exterior skin works well with the cloudy weather of Seattle, and the light colors are appropriate to the cityscape, which is surrounded by residential communities and natural landscape. With tall buildings interspersed throughout the downtown, the Washington Mutual Tower, with its proximity to the water and classical styling, emerges as a standout among the competition.

The main entrance to the building on the Third Street side leads to a formal lobby and elevator banks. Beyond the lobby a series of stairs and escalators descend to a three-story atrium which opens onto an outdoor plaza on the Second Street side. These elements serve as an internal transition linking the 35-foot grade difference between the two streets. Since it's easier to walk around the block and enter the building through the main entrance, the atrium is removed from the daily traffic of the building's users.

The outdoor plaza is defined by two low-rise buildings, one of which is the historic Brooklyn Building. The building's volume is determined by 30-foot-square corners which constitute the inner core. They are expressive elements on the exterior, in the form of piers which rise through the entire shaft of the building and contain vertical cylindrical bays which bulge from its center.

In plan, the shaft of the Tower is an overlapping square and circle, designed to create efficient office space. The top is cruciform in plan with the square corners of the shaft removed. The curved faces on each side are flattened with arched tops. The roof is capped with a pyramid surmounted by a lantern, reminiscent of 40 Wall Street.

Washington Mutual Tower

Location: Seattle, Washington, USA
Completion: 1988
Height: 735ft (224m)
Stories: 55
Area: 1.4 million ft²
Structure: Steel
Cladding: Granite, glass
Use: Office

2

3

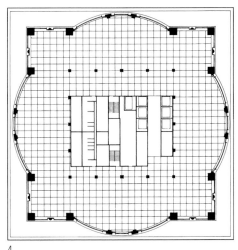

4

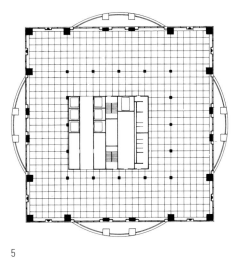

5

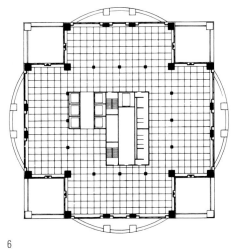

6

1 Historic Brooklyn Building stands in the foreground
   of Washington Mutual Tower (Opposite)
2 Seattle waterfront
3 Washington Mutual Tower
4–6 Typical floor plans
Photography: Charles Krebs courtesy Kohn Pedersen Fox
Associates PC (1); Cervin Robinson courtesy Kohn Pedersen
Fox Associates PC (2,3)

Architect: Kohn Pedersen Fox Associates PC
Associate Architect: The McKinley Architects
Structural Engineer: Kohn Pedersen Fox Associates PC
Services Engineer: Bouillon, Christopherson & Schairer
Owner/Developer: Wright Runstad & Company
General Contractor: Howard S. Wright Construction Co.

This 1.8 million-square-foot complex features not only a tower but also an annex with a banking hall, parking garage, and an athletic club. The two structures are connected by a glazed bridge over a landscaped plaza. The plaza features an attractively appointed retail space, benches, tables, and royal palm trees beneath a 12-story steel space frame. Both buildings are clad in a white thermal-finished granite.

The tower elevations have a grid overlay of black polished granite strips into which a large window is introduced. In turn, the window is divided into four equal lights that are framed in white and glazed with silver reflecting glass, creating an elaborate pattern of squares within squares. The annex structure employs the same materials (except for glass) in a different manner, incorporating pierced openings to facilitate garage ventilation.

The rectangular structure is supported by a composite tube frame. The southeast corner of the building features a cascade of receding cubes as the tower top turns away from neighboring buildings and faces the Biscayne Bay. The tower was designed to provide multiple views of the bay and the neighboring park. A consistent play of matte and reflective surfaces characterizes the project, along with the widespread use of pale marble flooring, simple woods, and a palette of clear colors. The fourth-floor auditorium features laminate walls with back-lit screens and an undulating, rough plaster ceiling which is designed with acoustics in mind.

Southeast Financial Center

Location: Miami, Florida, USA
Completion: 1983
Height: 738ft (224.9m)
Stories: 55
Area: 1.2 million ft²
Structure: Mixed
Cladding: Granite, marble, glass, metal
Use: Office

1 Southeast Financial Center (Opposite)
2 Receding cubes provide views of bay
3 Plaza framework
4 Auditorium
Photography: Esto courtesy Skidmore, Owings & Merrill (1-3); Esto (4)

4

Architect: Skidmore, Owings & Merrill (SOM)
Associate Architect: Ferendino, Grafton, Spillis & Candela
Structural Engineer: SOM
Services Engineer: I.A. Naman & Associates
Developer: Gerald D. Hines Interest and Southeast Bank, a partnership
General Contractor: Newberg, Duncan & Meyers

Built on land originally designated for government subsidized housing, the construction of the World Financial Center was said to symbolize the end of the recession of the 1970s for New York City. The riverfront landfill site is bounded by the Hudson River and the West Side Highway. Across this road are the World Trade Center Towers, which stand in contrast to the smaller reflective towers of the World Financial Center. Underground is criss-crossed with subway tubes and existing utility lines.

The developer was selected for its guarantee to complete the complex in record time—five years—while fulfilling the financial obligations associated with the redevelopment. After an invited competition, the architect was selected for his strong, contemporary, functional, and timeless design of a state-imposed master plan.

Designed to continue and celebrate the historic skyline of Manhattan, the complex includes four major towers ranging in height from 37 to 51 stories, topped with distinctive copper roofs. Two smaller towers act as a gateway to the riverside park surrounded by the towers. Between two of the towers is the winter garden, encased in a giant glass vault with exposed metal truss work. Ringed with retail stores, the stairs of the winter garden define a stage for special events. The complex also features connections to the World Trade Center's enclosed walkway across the West Side Highway.

The tallest of the four towers in a 14 1/2-acre development is Building C at 739 feet, home of the American Express Company. It is adjacent to the winter garden and connected to one of the enclosed walkways. All four towers rise from a continuous granite base. Zoning required setbacks that provided the transition from granite to glass in the shaft of the tower, while also designating the areas of entrance in the towers. Although lease requirements mandated changes throughout construction, the completed complex is very close to the original design.

The towers are supported by steel frames with braced cores which bear on a caisson foundation—with slurry walls for Building B—which then rests on bedrock. Columns visible in the lobbies, are 'sheathed in black to symbolize the serious work they are doing.' Hudson River water is used to cool the central mechanical plant of the complex. Revolving doors were installed in all lobbies to provide a thermal pressure seal between the buildings and the outside.

World Financial Center

Location: New York, New York, USA
Completion: 1985
Height: 739ft (225.3m)
Stories: 51
Area: 8.5 million ft² (entire complex)
Structure: Steel
Cladding: Granite, reflective glass
Use: Office

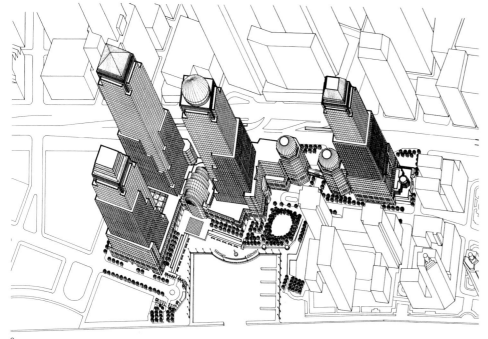

2

3

1 World Financial Center (Opposite)
2 Site plan
3 Multifaceted corners of World Financial Center
4 Sunrise in New York
Photography: Jeff Perkell courtesy Cesar Pelli & Associates (1,3);
Peter Aaron/Esto courtesy Cesar Pelli & Associates (4)

4

Architect: Cesar Pelli & Associates
Associate Architect: Adamson Associates
Structural Engineer: M.S. Yolles & Partners
Services Engineer: Flack & Kurtz
Developer: Olympia & York
General Contractor: Olympia & York

The Toronto-Dominion Centre, with the Toronto-Dominion Bank at its center, is located in the heart of the city's congested downtown business district, five blocks north of Lake Ontario and three blocks south of City Hall. Bounded by King, Bay, Wellington, and York Streets, the 5.5-acre site has direct vehicular access from three sides. The project called for 3.1 million gross square feet of office space (to be built in two stages), and a banking area of 22,500 square feet which would become the headquarters branch of the Toronto-Dominion Bank, replacing its old building on the same site. Also, specifications included shops, restaurants, a cinema, and extensive parking facilities to serve the general public and the Centre's own working population of 15,000 people.

Mies Van der Rohe served as consultant, and planned the composition of several great structures and open spaces. He was convinced that the banking functions required free and flexible space and decided to accommodate this complex function in a separate, single-story clear-span building and the two office towers, interlinked by public spaces and a plaza at the ground level. Below these plaza spaces, a shopping concourse was developed, connecting the towers with the banking pavillion. Below this is the parking facility.

The office tower is 124 x 244 feet. It has a structural steel frame and a structural bay 30 x 40 feet which accommodates the required elevators, stairs, and toilets in its service core. All around the service core, a column-free peripheral office space 40 feet deep facilitates optimum layouts. The 30 x 40 foot structural bay is divided into five-foot modular increments which provide flexibility.

In typical Miesian fashion, this building sets the dimensions of ceiling elements, including the combined fluorescent light and air handling fixtures, the peripheral induction units, and the location of the vertical mullion divisions of the building's outside skin. Steel mullions, spandrel plates and column covers are painted with matt black-baked finish and the glass is bronze-gray-tinted, heat absorbing and glare reflecting. There are three mechanical floors, each two stories in height, at the 14th, 43rd, and 56th floors. The ground floor lobby is gray granite. Core walls are faced with Roman travertine marble.

Toronto-Dominion Bank

Location: Toronto, Canada
Completion: 1967
Height: 740ft (225.6m)
Stories: 56
Area: 1.65 million ft²
Structure: Steel
Cladding: Gray granite, travertine marble
Use: Office

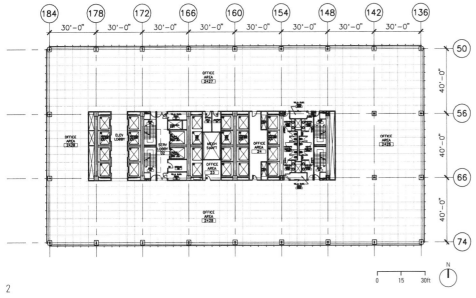

2

1 In the evening, lights shine brightly (Opposite)
2 Floor plan
3 View from ground level
4 Street entrance
5 Sculptures in public courtyard

Photography: Gary Beechey courtesy Bregman + Hamann Associates (1); Balthazar Korab Ltd courtesy Bregman + Hamann Associates (3); Ivan Zacnic (4,5)

3

4

5

Architects: Bregman + Hamann Associates and John B. Parkin Associates (in joint venture)
Consultant Architect: Mies Van der Rohe
Structural Engineer: Carruthers & Wallace Ltd
Services Engineer: H.H. Angus & Associates
Owners: Toronto-Dominion Bank/Cadillac Fairview Corporation
General Contractor: Pigott Construction Co. Ltd

The larger of two trapezoidal towers in the Wells Fargo Center complex, the Wells Fargo Bank Building at 740 feet tall is one of the many towers constructed under the Bunker Hill Redevelopment program which began in the mid-1970s to revitalize downtown Los Angeles. This surge in construction has grown to include such notable skyscrapers as First Interstate World Center, One California Plaza, Citicorp Plaza, and the Gas Company Tower.

Located over four acres, the 2.4-million-square-foot Wells Fargo Center complex also includes a second 45-story IBM Tower. These office towers are home to a number of prestigious banking, law, and business firms. Between the two towers is a three-story retail pavilion and interior court garden. This pavilion features 60,000 square feet of upscale restaurants and shops, as well as a three-million-dollar sculpture garden with lush greenery and water fountains. The anchor sculpture is a black aluminum and steel creation called 'Night Sail.' A tree-lined plaza links the two towers, while the center of the pavilion is enclosed in glass. The complex also includes the Wells Fargo Museum and over 2,000 on-site parking spaces.

Wells Fargo Bank, along with its neighboring IBM Tower, is sheathed in a rose-tone granite skin punctured by square, copper shaded glass. The 54-story building contains a total of 1.3 million square feet of usable space.

Wells Fargo Bank Building

(Formerly: Crocker Center)

Location: Los Angeles, California, USA
Completion: 1983
Height: 740ft (225.6m)
Stories: 54
Area: 1.3 million ft²
Structure: Steel
Cladding: Granite, glass
Use: Multiple

2

3

4

1   Wells Fargo Bank Building (right) and
    IBM Tower (left) (Opposite)
2   Ramps provide motorists with easy access to the towers
3   Pedestrian's view
4   Bunker Hill redevelopment
Photography: courtesy Skidmore, Owings & Merrill (1,2); Ivan Zaknic (3,4)

Architect: Skidmore, Owings & Merrill (SOM)
Landscape Architect: Lawrence Halprin
Structural Engineer: SOM
Associate Structural Engineer: Brandow & Johnson
    Associates
Mechanical Engineer: James A. Knowles
    & Associates
Developer: Maguire Thomas Partners

General Contractors: Henry C. Beck Company;
    Turner Construction Company

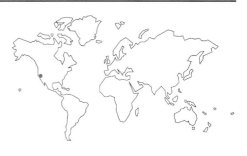

When it first opened in 1931, this bank and office building featured in its promotional advertisements the latest conveniences: "Every floor is provided with refrigerated water; all radiators are recessed; windows are plate glass; under-the-floor ducts; any desired outlets for telephones, lighting fixtures, or buzzers. The building is the very last word in all that spells DELUXE." Its roof had a brick promenade with 360 degree views that, back in its early years, was accessible at a cost of 50 cents per visitor. "No one visiting New York should fail to visit the 'City Bank Farmers Trust' edifice—this magnificent and beautiful pile of marble, stone, and masonry..."

This quintessentially modern-age building was once the second tallest tower in lower Manhattan and the fourth tallest in the world. Today it is one of the city's most overlooked historical skyscrapers.

The building occupies the entire block bounded by Exchange Place, William, Beaver, and Hanover Streets. Its classic setback design provides various floor areas ranging from approximately 20,000 square feet at the lowest floors to about 5,000 square feet at the top floors. 20 Exchange Place continues its tradition of keeping up with all the modern conveniences, offering high-speed elevators, acoustical ceilings, and full air-conditioning. The showcase of the building is its 30-foot-high marble lobby crowned by a stepped dome and supported by sculpted marble columns.

The plan of the building was determined entirely by the requirements of the two banking institutions that were to use it at the time, and by its irregular site in the heart of a very congested area. The banks required two primary entrances, and the elevators were placed at the center so that there would be no interruption of shafts to the top of the tower.

In its details, the interior public spaces—such as a gracefully curving stair leading to a barrel-vaulted senior officer's room, and the unusual white-metal crafted ornamental grilles, air intakes, directories and elaborate elevator doors—give this architectural ensemble the strength and fluidity of the Art Deco style, popular in that period.

In a single ground floor banking room, rich materials were used to create a solid sense of luxury in a public place, designed to communicate the message that all in capitalism was not lost—even at the height of the Great Depression.

20 Exchange Place

(Formerly: City Bank Farmers Trust Building)

Location: New York, New York, USA
Completion: 1931
Height: 741ft (225.9m)
Stories: 57
Area: Approx. 500,000 ft²
Structure: Steel
Cladding: Marble, stone
Use: Office

2

3

4

5

1   View from ground level (Opposite)
2   View of 20 Exchange Place in the Manhattan skyline
3   Art Deco lobby
4   Detail
5   Art Deco lobby
Photography: Douglas Mason (1,3,4,5); Ivan Zaknic (2)

Architect: Cross & Cross
Builder: George Fuller Construction Co.

With a view of Malaysia and Indonesia and overlooking the seaside city of Singapore, the Westin Stamford Hotel was the tallest hotel in the world and the tallest building in Southeast Asia at the time of its construction. Conceived in 1969, it took another 17 years to reach completion.

This unique building is part of Raffles City, one of the world's largest mixed-use developments under single ownership. Surrounded by commercial, historical, and cultural monuments, this four-million-square-foot complex was undertaken as the centerpiece of a program to invigorate the downtown after business hours.

The Raffles development, a self-contained 'city within a city,' consists of four separate towers, including a 42-story office building and two hotels: the 73-story Westin Stamford with 1,253 guest rooms and an 800-room hotel in twin 28-story towers. All of the towers rise from a seven-story podium housing a multi-tiered atrium, or skylit town plaza, ringed by shops, restaurants, and lounges. The podium's landscaped roof holds a pool, tennis courts, and other recreational facilities. Below the podium are three parking levels and operational utilities.

Rather than attempt to integrate this very large development with the smaller-scale buildings that surround it, contextualism was sought through massing and complementary contrast. Apparent bulk is diminished by positioning the tallest building in relation to the grassy *padang*, the largest open space available, and by twisting the entire complex 45 degrees so that it meets the street obliquely (a strategy that protects the viewer from confronting a flat wall at every street corner). Westin Stamford Hotel, rising 741 feet, shifts in appearance from the cylindrical to the rectangular as the observer's viewpoint changes.

To avoid the need for a pile foundation more than 130 feet deep, which would have added several months of construction time, the contractor used a mat foundation up to 16 feet thick, the thickest part of which is under the tallest of the four towers.

The structure is of reinforced concrete beams, joists and slabs spanning from the perimeter columns to the core, leaving the interior spaces column-free. In contrast with the neighboring stucco and tile buildings, the curtain walls are aluminum with predominantly tinted glass except for the ground floor, where clear glass was used. The hotel has a 'double facade' with the inner wall at the plane of the sliding glass doors and the outer walls with punched aluminum panels at the terrace edges.

Westin Stamford Hotel

(Also known as: Raffles City)

Location: Singapore
Completion: 1986
Height: 741ft (225.9m)
Stories: 73
Area: 1.16 million ft²
Structure: Mixed
Cladding: Aluminium, tinted and clear glass
Use: Multiple

2

3

4

5

1 View of Raffles City's four skyscrapers (Opposite)
2 Multi-tiered plaza
3 Shoppers and hotel guests navigate the many levels
4 Skylit atrium
5 Entrance
Photography: Shang Wei Kouo courtesy Pei Cobb
Freed & Partners

Architect: I.M. Pei & Partners
Associate Architect: Architects 61
Structural Engineer: Weiskopf & Pickworth, with
**   Sim Bee Tek & Associates**
Services Engineer: Consentini Associates with
**   CMP Consulting Pte. Ltd**
Developer: Raffles City (Pte.) Ltd
General Contractor: Ssangyong Construction Co. Ltd

On what was once the site of a Greyhound bus terminal, rises a subtle skyscraper, designed as twin towers, with 2.3 million square feet of space. The Chicago Title and Trust Center is a work in progress with only the first phase complete, which includes one of the towers and the base of the building. The tower is really two distinct buildings, joined by a low-rise base. With the base related to the building's neighbors and the tower related to the skyline, the building is unified by its materials and detailing.

The base is scaled to relate to its low-rise neighbors, the Illinois State Office Building and the historic City Hall-County Building designed by Holabird and Root. The height of the base was determined by the adjacent Daley Center, and it features separate entrances on the sides for the towers with the low-rise Title Center section in the middle. A skylit, retail galleria connects the three lobbies, and underground pedestrian tunnels connect to public mass transportation and the State of Illinois Center across the street.

The tower is designed to emphasize its slender verticality against the rather monumental base. The front facade is articulated in strips of glass and metal, while glass step-backs at the corners, create the transition to the Sardinian white-flamed granite and glass of the sides. White aluminum accents the recessed windows and top. The white finishes and clear glass allow the tower to have a softer, more delicate impact on its surroundings, especially in comparison with the dark-skinned behemoths which dominate Chicago. The top of the building features a sculptural glass and metal crown.

Construction utilized the existing buildings' foundations and framing as a retention wall, thus shaving five months off the schedule. This method allowed for the simultaneous construction of the core and steel framing up to the 20th floor and down to the four underground parking levels and exterior foundations. Construction also featured a 20-foot tall barricade painted to resemble a child's set of toy building blocks. The developer and Tyco, manufacturer of toy blocks, donated actual building blocks to neighboring daycare centers in a goodwill gesture.

Chicago Title and Trust Center

Location: Chicago, Illinois, USA
Completion: 1993 (one tower)
Height: 742ft (226.2m)
Stories: 50
Area: 1.2 million ft² (one tower)
Structure: Steel
Cladding: Glass, metal, stone
Use: Office

2

3

1 Chicago Title and Trust Center (Opposite)
2 View of rooftop floors
3 Clarke Street entrance
4 Elevation from Couch Place
Photography: Barbara Karant (1,2,3)

4

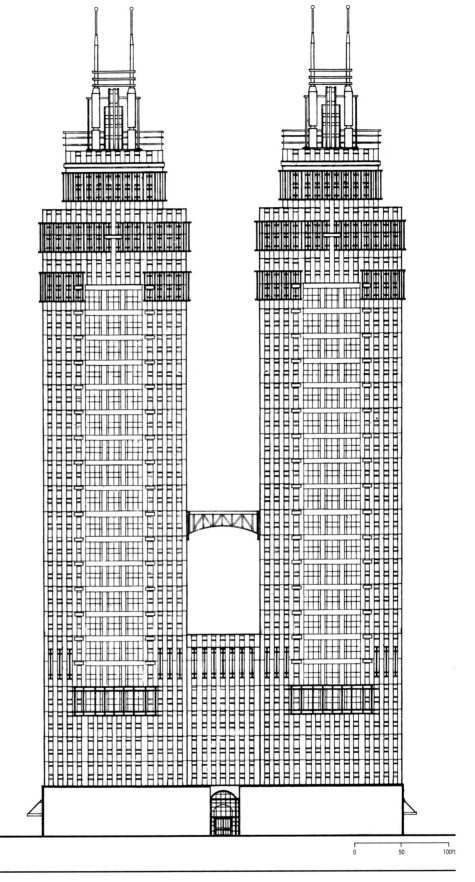

0   50   100ft

Architect: Kohn Pederson Fox Associates PC
Structural Engineer: Severud-Szegezdy
Services Engineer: Environmental Systems Design
Developer: The Linpro Company
General Contractor: Morse Diesel Construction Co.

Sunshine 60 is one element in a much larger complex. The flagship of a massive, unprecedented urban redevelopment program, the tower was the tallest building in Japan at the time of its completion in 1978.

The redevelopment complex is really a 'city within a city' which, along with the Sunshine 60 office tower, features apartments, commercial spaces, cultural facilities, and urban public spaces (including parks and gardens). The complex also features convenient access to major highways and the public transit systems. The tower itself is adjacent to a park and a three-story, skylit retail mall. An 11-story department store, 36-story hotel, and 12-story bus terminal and cultural facility round out the group.

Floors 10–57 are office spaces. On the lower floors workers have access to a post office, banks, showrooms, cafeterias, a health care center, and a daycare center. The 58th and 59th floors feature restaurants with spectacular views. From the 60th-floor observation deck, visitors can see as far as 100km on a clear day. The observation deck is served by an elevator directly from the lobby that travels 600 meters per minute; the entire trip skyward takes a mere 35 seconds.

The tower is served by a total of 40 elevators. The rooftop floor is for mechanical equipment, placed directly above the core of the building.

The foundation is reinforced concrete, the lower part of the tower is reinforced concrete with steel skeleton and the tower portion is steel skeleton with slitted walls. These unique slitted walls were inserted between columns in the core. The walls can thus conform to deformations in the steel frame caused by earthquakes and wind shear, and help maintain the structural integrity of the building. The frame is a tube-in-tube structural system. The exterior of the building reflects this system with columns of steel interspersed with glass.

Sunshine 60

(Formerly: Ikebukuro Tower)

Location: Tokyo, Japan
Completion: 1978
Height: 742ft (226.2m)
Stories: 60
Area: 2.6 million ft²
Structure: Mixed
Cladding: Steel, glass
Use: Office

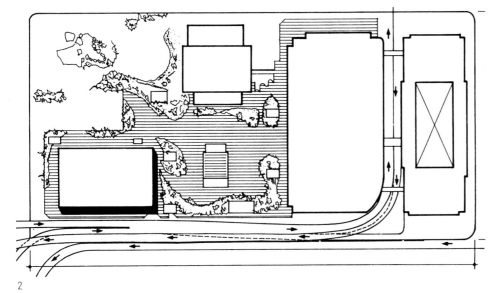

1 View of Sunshine 60 (Opposite)
2 Site plan
3 Mechanical and machine rooms atop the roof
4 Typical floor plan
Photography: courtesy Sunshine City Corporation (1);
Kousi Miwa courtesy Mitsubishi Estate Co. Ltd. (3)

2

3

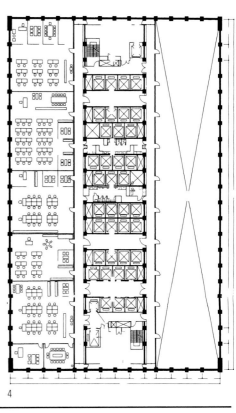

4

Architect: Mitsubishi Estate Co. Ltd
Structural Engineer: Muto Institute of Structural
   Mechanics Inc.
Services Engineer: Mitsubishi Estate Co. Ltd
Developer: The Japan Urban Development Co. Ltd
General Contractors: Kajima Corporation, Shimizu
   Construction Co. Ltd, Tokyo Construction Co. Ltd
   (a joint venture)

Featuring an elaborate public plaza at its base and a 2,500-car underground garage, this granite-clad square tower was designed to enhance not only the daily life of its estimated 8,000 inhabitants, but also its surrounding community.

The tower's orientation on the site serves functional as well as aesthetic purposes. Its positioning at a 45-degree angle to the street grid improves sun shading, which lowers lighting, heating, and air-conditioning costs. Inside the tower are thirty elevators. The concourse level features a 200-seat auditorium, 750-seat cafeteria, restaurant, and retail spaces. The first fully-sprinklered high-rise in Los Angeles county, the tower was also designed to meet or exceed all known earthquake design criteria and features a rooftop helipad as required by code. The tower was designed to serve the bank's needs until the year 2000.

Outside the building on the rest of the site, is a lavish 3.5-acre, two-level public garden which is landscaped and decorated with sculptures. The main entrance is reached by a series of steps in a semi-circular design leading to the main level of the plaza and 50-foot-high sculpture. The northern portion of the complex features smaller gardens composed around a semi-circular fountain. Pedestrian bridges over most of the bordering streets provide safe access for the occupants, while ensuring less congestion for motorists.

333 South Hope Building

(Formerly: Security Pacific Plaza)

Location: Los Angeles, California, USA
Completion: 1975
Height: 743ft (226.5m)
Stories: 55
Area: 1.7 million ft²
Structure: Steel
Cladding: Granite
Use: Office

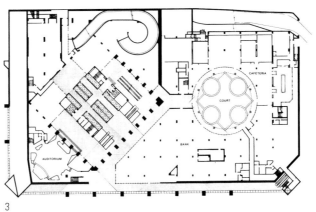

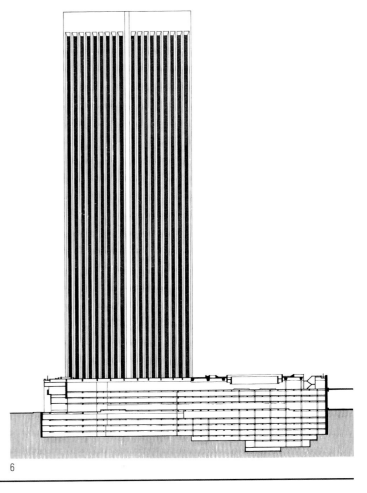

1 View of 333 South Hope Building (Opposite)
2 Foyer looking out at Los Angeles skyline
3 Concourse level plan
4 Public courtyard
5 Semi-circular fountain with gardens
6 Section looking south
Photography: Wayne Thom courtesy Albert C. Martin & Associates (1,5); Don Higgins (2); Ivan Zacnic (4)

2

4

5

6

Architect: Albert C. Martin & Associates
Structural Engineer: Albert C. Martin & Associates
Services Engineer: Albert C. Martin & Associates
Developer: Security Pacific Bank
General Contractor: Turner Construction Co.
Landscape Architect: Sasaki, Walker Associates, Inc.

Located in the heart of New York's Wall Street area, on a two-block site near the World Trade Center, One Liberty Plaza clearly expresses its steel structure and utilizes the latest technology. Soon after its completion in 1973, the tower was awarded the American Institute of Steel Construction's coveted architectural award of excellence. The award called attention to the unique features of the building, among which is its 'completely column-free office floor layout facilitating some of the most functional, imaginative, and magnificent installations to be found anywhere.'

U.S. Steel, in joint venture with Galbreath-Ruffin Corporation, wanted an exemplary building with the main emphasis on the structural aspects but also one that integrated lighting, air-conditioning, and vertical transportation. Before settling on this design, nine prototype structural designs, all based on a column-free plan, were analyzed for cost and other considerations. The selected design uses the fire-proofed flanges to protect the unfireproofed web, providing a significant savings in cladding material. Another cost advantage was the 6-foot, 3-inch-deep girders, which provide a 50% column connection, allowing a major part of the wind force to be taken by the exterior frame.

Through a special zoning waiver, the designers were permitted to consolidate all the allowable floor area on the larger block, leaving the smaller block for a public amenity in the form of a park. The park and its surrounding plaza are integrated by large steps at each end of the plaza for seating, since the site slopes approximately 10 feet downward from Broadway toward Church Street.

The building has a gross floor area of 2.13 million square feet including about 128,000 square feet in the two stories below the plaza. From the first level below the plaza, connected with the lobby by escalators, pedestrian passages lead to subway stations and to the World Trade Center. The pedestrian connection was part of a comprehensive pedestrian circulation system in the special Greenwich Street Development district, one of several pedestrian systems approved by the New York City Zoning Commission in the early 1970s.

In 1989, the plaza and lobby underwent renovation, repairs, and expansion.

One Liberty Plaza

(Also known as: U.S. Steel Building)

Location: New York, New York, USA
Completion: 1973
Height: 743ft (226.5m)
Stories: 54
Area: 2.13 million ft²
Structure: Steel
Cladding: Exposed steel
Use: Office

3

4

5

7

CORTLANDT STREET

CHURCH STREET

BROADWAY

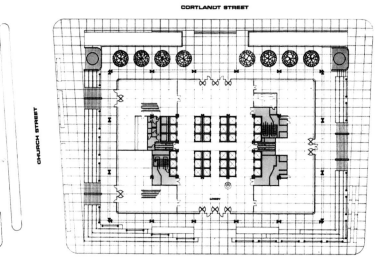

LIBERTY STREET

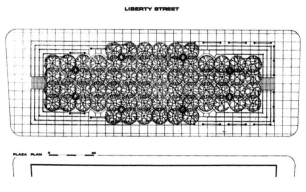

PLAZA PLAN

6

1&2   One Liberty Plaza (Opposite)
   3   View from the street
   4   One Liberty Plaza contrasts and complements its older
       neighbors
   5   Steel is fully expressed
   6   Site plan
   7   Entrance

Photography: Douglas Mason (1,7); Esto courtesy Skidmore,
Owings & Merrill (2,5); Esto (3,4)

Architect: Skidmore, Owings & Merrill
Structural Engineers: Paul Weidlinger in association
with Weiskopf & Pickworth
Services Engineer: Syska & Hennessy
Developers: Galbreath-Ruffin Corporation,
in association with U.S. Steel Corporation
General Contractor: Turner Construction Company

Structural Steel Fabricator/Erector: American Bridge
Division, U.S. Steel Corp.

41

Two Union Square is a multi-use complex that consists of a 56-story tower, a retail court, and enclosed public spaces. The tower is basically a crystalline box with applied regular and irregular curved forms, through which the architects recalled sails and ships, mountains and lakes, and even the region's dominant industries: aeronautics and marine products.

Although the tower is simple in form, its skin has many subtle details. The ochre-colored vertical and horizontal lines of a 'supergrid' on all glass facades serve to provide scale reference and to relate the tower to the ochre-colored columns at its base, while curving horizontal spandrels on the facades add to its slender proportions.

Virtually column-free interior space results in open flexible floor plans, and up to 10 corner offices per floor with unobstructed views to Seattle's skyline. Twenty-two high-speed elevators carry passengers directly to all floors without transfer.

The parking garage, one of the largest in Seattle with its four underground levels, provides over 1,100 parking spaces, while the Convention Center next door provides an additional 1,000 spaces. Two Union Square is connected to the Convention Center, Freeway Park, and other downtown buildings through an underground concourse and other weather-protected walkways. The three-level courtyard covers an acre of exterior space and serves as a 'living room for the city.'

The main pedestrian space features a cascading mountain stream, three public fountains, a wide spectrum of plants and an outdoor amphitheater. This outdoor space was designed to capture midday sun year-round and welcome passers-by to its more tranquil and reflective environment.

The developer of Two Union Square did not want the exterior or interior bracing to obstruct the views and preferred to feature the glazed corners, free of structure. This solution required the highest strength concrete ever used in a building: 19,000 psi throughout the entire 56 stories.

The structure relies on four 10-foot-diameter steel cylinders which define the building core and support nearly half of the floor loads on each level. These cylinders are filled with high-strength concrete, and tubes are connected by a composite spandrel beam to 14 concrete columns along the perimeter of the building. Because these columns are of high-strength concrete, their size could be reduced and the need for intermediate columns eliminated. The same strength concrete was used to limit motion due to wind forces. The combination of steel and concrete led to about a 30% savings in cost.

Two Union Square

Location: Seattle, Washington, USA
Completion: 1989
Height: 743ft (226.5m)
Stories: 56
Area: 1.2 million ft²
Structure: Mixed
Cladding: Glass
Use: Multiple

2

3

4

5

6

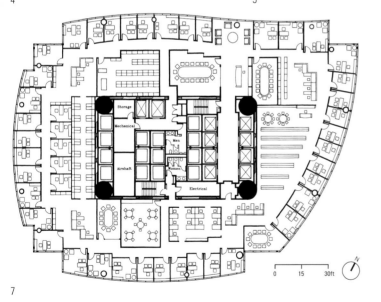
7

1 Two Union Square, view from the west (Opposite)
2 Courtyard with wave-form benches, details of earlier building on this site
3 Courtyard entrance from west
4 Exterior walkway, north side at lobby level
5 Forest-like elevator lobby with dappled light
6 View from the east at dusk
7 Typical office floor plan
Photography: Peter Hursley courtesy The NBBJ Group (1-6)

0   15   30ft

Architect: The NBBJ Group
Structural Engineer: Skilling Ward Magnusson Berkshire, Inc.
Services Engineer: Bouillon Christofferson and Schairer, Inc.
Developer: Unico Properties, Inc.
General Contractor: Turner Construction

At first sight, the Governor Phillip Tower, a 64-story office building in Sydney, appears to be a block of granite resting on a base of zinc. A closer look reveals that the Tower is sitting on a massive beam clad in zinc and resting on a sandstone base, which houses the impressive loggia and a foyer of grand proportions.

The zinc-clad beams act visually to separate the Tower from the sandstone-clad podium base and make stylistic reference in material and detail to the metal roofscape on the historic sandstone buildings within the precinct. The expression of the Tower as a polished granite and stainless steel block set on a sandstone plinth evolved from the constraints of the site, where a heightened contrast between the old handcrafted masonry and the more recent machine-cut materials was considered essential.

The facade is polished Paradiso granite, light gray in color with a blue/pink hue, displaying warm layers of sandstone color. Metal inlays on the surface define a three-story grid on the facade, leading to the dramatic termination of the Tower by a six-story grid of stainless steel blades which appear to extend from inside the structure.

The podium is designed as a traditional masonry building, clad in sandstone and granite, and detailed with inlays of metal. Even though the facade is contemporary, it relates to the traditional sandstone facades of the area as well. This impressive and solid-looking mass is perforated by windows, entrances, and colonnades. Access to the office Tower is from a new public place created by closing the southern end of Young Street and integrating Farrer Place by extensive landscaping and paving.

The entrance from Farrer Place is through a loggia, which takes the form of a spacious gallery leading to the foyers of Governor Phillip Tower and a neighboring Governor Macquarie Tower, and a through-site link to an alternative entrance on Phillip Street.

Inside the loggia, the finish echoes the sandstone seen on the outside of the podium. The foyer of the Tower is a gallery-like space, rising to 16 meters with a glazed roof, through which can be seen the transfer beams upon which the Tower rests. The natural light during the day from the glass roof creates an impressive feeling over this vast area. The finish of the foyer also reflects the exterior of the building. Sculptures and other works of art have been commissioned to enhance even further this elegant foyer.

Governor Phillip Tower

Location: Sydney, Australia
Completion: 1993
Height: 745ft (227.1m)
Stories: 64
Area: 592,000 ft²
Structure: Mixed
Cladding: Sandstone, granite
Use: Office

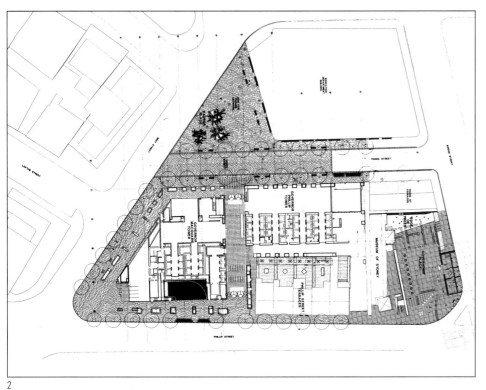

1 Governor Phillip Tower slices the sky with its angular top
   (Opposite)
2 Site plan with first floor layout
3 Architectural details
4 Under construction
5 Foyer
6 Elevation
Photography: John Gollings courtesy Denton Corker
Marshall Pty Ltd

2

3

4

5

6

Architect: Denton Corker Marshall Pty Ltd
Structural Engineer: Ove Arup & Partners
Services Engineer: TWA Consultants
Developers: State Authorities Superannuation Board
General Contractor: Grocon Limited (GPT & GMT)

Many buildings in the Financial District of New York were constructed in the early part of the century. Most are assertive, distinguished in form and bold in scale. For 60 Wall Street, home of J.P. Morgan and Company, the architects interpreted freely from the language of classical architecture, employing the full range of compositional elements.

The site is at mid-block across from a landmark building at 55 Wall Street dating from 1842, which was originally built as the Merchant's Exchange and later used as New York's Custom House. Through the city's special permit process, 365,000 square feet of airspace were acquired and transferred from this landmark to 60 Wall Street. Another 160,000 extra square feet were authorized by the zoning in return for providing an outdoor plaza for pedestrians.

The design of the building addressed the historical context and the challenge of making the tower functional and contemporary with all of its communication systems, energy efficiency and computerized interior spaces. The classical tripartite subdivision into the base, shaft and capital was employed: a distinctive public space at street level, the tower, and the termination in a mansard-shaped roof. The building's major portion, the tower, sits on a four-story base or podium which fills most of the site, and reflects through its height the cornice lines of the neighboring buildings. A 70-foot-high colonnade of double columns line both streets, recalling the Greek Revival facade of its distinguished neighbor at 55 Wall Street. The three floors above ground, each measuring 54,000 square feet with high ceilings, are all almost column-free, and used for trading activities.

Above the base, corner-shafts continue the motif of the colonnade in a pattern of ribbon window layers to give the illusion of the bundled pilasters of each corner with a curtain wall stretched between. The green and pink granite used at the base is repeated for the horizontal bands of the tower. At the 42nd floor, the corner projections provide a base for a special eight-story pilaster containing stacked bay windows, which in turn is surmounted by the 40-foot-high mansard roof containing mechanical systems behind it, including microwave and satellite communications equipment.

Construction is steel frame with clear spans for the rentable space. The exterior finishes consist of antique silver reflecting glass and gray-and-green granite spandrels, and mullions at street level in bronze and bronze painted aluminum above.

At street level the building contains a three-story-high half-acre public indoor park. Here the public finds fountains and boxed trees, mounds of greenery, latticework, glass canopies, flowers, waterfalls, kiosks and cafes. These public areas provide a needed place of relaxation and peace, a respite from the bustle of the surrounding city.

J.P. Morgan Headquarters

Location: New York, New York, USA
Completion: 1992
Height: 745ft (227.1m)
Stories: 56
Area: 106 million ft²
Structure: Steel
Cladding: Reflecting glass, granite, bronze, aluminum
Use: Office

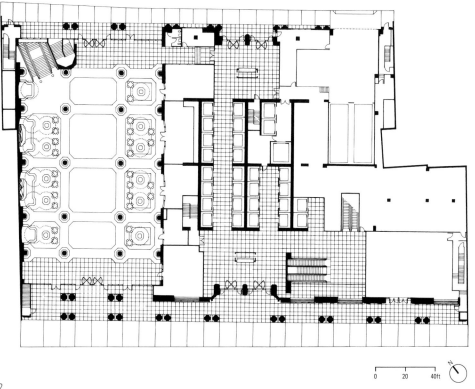

2

3

5

4

1 J.P. Morgan Headquarters (Opposite)
2 Ground floor plan
3 View of building
4 Street entrance
5 Roof construction
Photography: Livieri-KRJDA courtesy Kevin Roche, John
Dinkeloo and Associates (1,3,4,5)

Architects: Kevin Roche, John Dinkeloo
   and Associates
Structural Engineer: The Office of Irwin G. Cantor
Services Engineer: Syska & Hennessy
Developer: Park Tower Group
General Contractor: Tishman Construction
   Corp. of N.Y.

This 55-story, granite clad office tower, with two additional levels below grade, contains approximately 1.9 million square feet of space and covers two city blocks. The clients—Houston Oil and Minerals and the First International Bank—required a world headquarters' office building to provide space for their expanding organizations, and occupy 67% of the building.

The program requirements called for an international banking office, headquarters' office space, and restaurant facilities both for the public and for employees. A typical floor contains 22,000 square feet of rentable space. Twenty-seven passenger elevators serve the tower.

A bank securities department, convenience shops, a restaurant, and small auditorium are located on the concourse level, which is below the plaza but which enters at grade by taking advantage of the sloping site. An attached banking lobby and a 106-foot-high roof is formed by a series of 15-foot setbacks.

At the top, one side moves inward in seven steps. The tower was conceived as a sculptural form, using bay windows, setbacks, and highly reflective surfaces of polished carnelian granite and bronze glass. Adjacent buildings and views of the city influenced the siting of the building. Fifty percent of the site is left as open space, forming an urban plaza for the city. The plaza features the 'Monument au Fantome.'

The structural system consists of a 'serrated exterior composite tube' system with columns at intervals of 10 feet. The tube is made up of 44-inch wide columns and 46-inch deep spandrels at each floor. Floor framing consists of steel wide-flange beams, 10 feet on center, with two-inch metal deck and a three-and-a-quarter inch lightweight concrete slab. The entire lateral wind load on the building is taken by the exterior tube. The structure rests on a mat foundation which extends approximately 45 feet below grade.

1100 Louisiana Building

(Formerly: Interfirst Plaza)

Location: Houston, Texas
Completion: 1980
Height: 748ft (228m)
Stories: 55
Area: 1.9 million ft²
Structure: Mixed
Cladding: Carnelian granite, bronze glass
Use: Office

1 1100 Louisiana Building (Opposite)
2 Jagged facade
3 Sculpted form of 1100 Louisiana Building
4 View from ground level
Photography: Skidmore, Owings & Merrill (1,2);
Hedrich-Blessing courtesy Skidmore, Owings & Merrill (3,4)

2

Architect: Skidmore, Owings & Merrill
Associate Architect: 3D/International
Mechanical Engineer: I.A. Naman and Associates
Developers: Gerald D. Hines Interests & Prudential
  Insurance Company (PIC) Realty Corporation
Contractor: W.S. Bellows Construction Co.

Located in the southern outskirts of Seoul in the Kang Nam area, this project was the subject of a limited international competition held in September, 1984. Adjacent to the city's Olympic Stadium, the tower was built by the Korean Traders Association on the occasion of the Olympic Games held in Seoul in 1988.

The complex is on a site of approximately 190,000 square meters, and incorporates the headquarters of the Association and other related facilities: an 800-room hotel, an exhibition center, the air terminal for passengers using Seoul International Airport, a shopping center, and a parking lot for 3,000 cars.

The tower proper, 54 stories high with two basement levels, is called the Korea World Trade Center building, occupying a total floor area of 1.16 million square feet. Stepping back equally four times as it rises, this building dramatically towers above the low Seoul skyline. It is clad in locally produced reflective glass, mirroring the blue sky and minimizing the bulk impact of the building. A sunken tree-lined public plaza with restaurants and shops provides pedestrian activity. A fountain is situated at the end of the plaza near the tower.

In Korea, the ground is so hard that excavation takes extra time; therefore, underground work is allowed to start before the building permit is issued. In many cases, construction is started in the winter when underground water is frozen, as a means of controlling underground water. In the case of the Korean World Trade Center, since it is on a large, wide site, open overall excavation was made without earth retaining walls, and concreting proceeded from the lowermost basement level upwards, except that the rock foundation had some fissures, raising some problem of bearing capacity of the ground. As a result of research, poured-in-situ piles of 3.5 and 1.5 meters in diameter were used. This proved to be very difficult work because the rock formations had to be hollowed out to 3.5 meters diameter to the depth of 12.3 meters.

At 748 feet, Korea World Trade Center is the second tallest in the city of Seoul, and second tallest in Korea itself, to the Korea Life Insurance Company at 817 feet. Its design, according to the structural engineer, "symbolized the appearance of two stone Buddhist images standing on both sides of the gate of the Korean temple, originally wishing safe launching out as a country of international trade." However, as the building took shape gradually, people began to see different images in its design—a rising dragon, and a 'straight-line connected graph showing Korea's growth of export, sometimes referred to as the miracle of Hang Gang.'

Korea World Trade Center

Location: Seoul, Korea
Completion: 1988
Height: 748ft (228m)
Stories: 54
Area: 1.16 million ft²
Structure: Steel
Cladding: Reflective glass
Use: Multiple

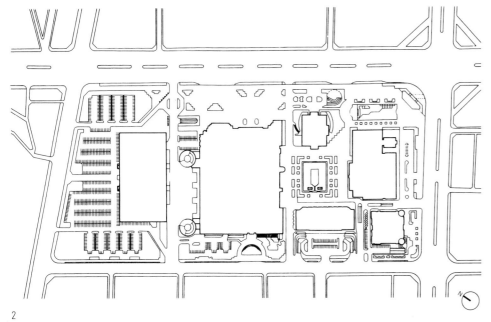

2

4

3

1 Korea World Trade Center (Opposite)
2 Site plan
3 Sunken plaza
4 Reflective glass facade
Photography: Park Young Chae courtesy Nikken Sekkei Ltd
(1); Kiyohiko Higashide courtesy Nikken Sekkei Ltd (3,4)

**Architect: Hsin-Yieh Architects & Associates
    Architects Group and Junglim Architects
    and Engineers
Structural Engineer: Nikken Sekkei Ltd
    in association with Wondosi
Services Engineer: Nikken Sekkei Ltd
Developer: Korean Foreign Trade Association**

On a sloping wooded site which was once home to British forces, there stand several modern towers, a podium retail space, and Hong Kong Park. The site was divided into four lots by the Hong Kong Government—one for itself, one for the park, and two for commercial development. The developer bought both commercial properties at auction.

Construction of the complex was divided into two phases. Phase One comprised a podium for shops and cinemas, garden court, and two rectangular-shaped towers. The two elliptical towers atop the six-story retail podium were built during Phase Two. The two phases are linked by a landscaped park lane at the podium level. The podium features a Banyan tree original to the site, which is preserved in the 'world's largest flower pot.'

The entire Pacific Place complex includes three hotels, two apartment buildings, two office developments, the Mall (one of Hong Kong's largest), and parking. There are direct connections to a mass transit railway station and local highways, as well as pedestrian bridges across surrounding roadways and an escalator connection between Queensway and Hong Kong Park.

The first elliptical tower is One Pacific Place, containing the Conrad Hilton and Parkside Apartments. The tallest tower of the complex, Two Pacific Place, also called Island Shangri-La Tower, is divided into two parts. The Island Shangri-la Hotel occupies the upper 18 floors with six hundred rooms arranged around a central atrium. The lower 27 floors contain more than 700,000 square feet of office space.

The architecture and engineering of the complex is simple and elegant, designed to unify the various functions. The interior of the hotel has been described as a unique and varied style of flamboyant baroque.

Two Pacific Place/Island Shangri-La Hotel

Location: Hong Kong
Completion: 1991
Height: 748ft (228m)
Stories: 56
Area: Approx. 1.15 million ft²
Structure: Concrete
Cladding: Concrete, glass
Use: Multiple

3

4

5

2

1   *Two Pacific Place/Island Shangri-La Hotel (center) is*
    joined by Conrad Hilton (left) and J.W. Marriott Hotel (right)
2   *Aerial view of entire Pacific Place complex*
3   *Glass entrance way*
4   *Landscaped atrium*
5   *View of mall*
Photography: courtesy Wong & Ouyang (HK) Ltd

Architect: Wong & Ouyang (HK) Ltd
Structural Engineer: Wong & Ouyang (HK) Ltd
Services Engineer: Wong & Ouyang (HK) Ltd
Developer: Swire Properties

The Gas Company Tower, along with the First Interstate World Center, were the key pieces for the developer in the Bunker Hill Restoration Project of Los Angeles. The rights to build these mammoth structures were purchased from the adjacent Central Library. Funds from the purchase were used to renovate and preserve the Central Library and Pershing Square on the other side of the Gas Company Tower. The base of the Tower serves as a link between the library and the square.

The height of the Tower base is constructed to match the nearby Biltmore Hotel. The base contains three entrance lobbies connected by escalators, stairs, elevators, internal streets and hanging gardens. The proportions of the Pershing Square entrance, which stands 60 feet above the Central Library entrance, are designed to relate to the openness of an adjoining park.

The Gas Company Tower's form responds to its neighboring towers, not in imitation, but rather through employing a similar 'language.' The central shaft of the Tower, clad in granite with punched openings, is similar to the nearby Arco Tower. The sides, as in the First Interstate World Center next door, are sheathed in a metallic skin. The elliptical blue glass volume that penetrates the blue-gray granite of the shaft was inspired by a gas flame, while its reflectivity distinguishes it from the shaft of the Tower. As the Tower rises, the shaft reduces until only the blue glass remains, inside of which is hidden mechanical units and an emergency helipad.

The structure of the Tower consists of a combination of steel elements. The perimeter columns spaced on 15-foot centers support the shaft of the Tower while providing column-free interiors. At the base, the loads of alternate columns were transferred by five-story-tall vierendeel girders to the main columns, which helps the Tower resist lateral loads. The broad sides are constructed with ductile moment frames while the other faces consist of braced frames and moment frames which utilize outrigger girders. The combination of these systems provides the necessary lateral resistance to the forces of wind and earthquake, while supporting the vertical loads imposed by gravity.

Gas Company Tower

Location: Los Angeles, California, USA
Completion: 1991
Height: 749ft (228.3m)
Stories: 54
Area: 1.4 million ft²
Structure: Steel
Cladding: Granite, aluminum panels, reflective glass, metal
Use: Office

2

3

4

5

6

1 Gas Company Tower (Opposite)
2 View from ground level
3 Architectural details
4 Foyer
5 Elevator lobby
6 Entrance to Gas Company Tower
Photography: courtesy CBM Engineers, Inc. (1);
Bruce Stewart (2); Skidmore, Owings & Merrill (3,4,5,6)

Architect: Skidmore, Owings & Merrill
Structural Engineer: CBM Engineers, Inc.
Services Engineer: James A. Knowles & Associates
Developer: Maguire Thomas Partners
General Contractor: Turner Construction Company

Rising 750 feet from a six-story base, 1251 Avenue of the Americas is the second-tallest structure in Rockefeller Center. Once the global headquarters of Exxon Corporation, today it is home and headquarters to many other distinguished organizations including prominent leaders in finance, banking, and law.

The 54-story building occupies 96,300 square feet of the site. It is set back from the Avenue of the Americas by a 100-foot-deep, open landscaped plaza with a two-tiered pool—the largest for a commercial building in New York City.

The tower expresses strong verticality through its design and the materials used. The sheer facade of vertical limestone piers is a prime example of the late International-style architecture that dominated the Manhattan skyline in the late 1960s and 1970s. Its striking lines are accentuated by alternating tiers of glass and bronze-tinted aluminum; at the sidewalk, dramatic canopies are cantilivered to protect the buildings' entrances on both 49th and 50th Streets.

The lobby design and lighting were reworked in 1993. The bronze basket-weave pattern echoes the original patterns found in Rockefeller Center's other buildings with their Art Deco heritage. The lobby occupies the entire ground floor and is sheathed in Italian marble with terrazzo floors; the 30-foot-high ceiling is provided with custom-designed lighting. The lobby walls are full-height windows crowned by six-foot-high art glass. At the rear of the lobby, a retail corridor connects to the bank, restaurant and retail space with a mezzanine.

Escalators carry pedestrians to lower levels of the Concourse connected with the Rockefeller Center underground concourse and a subway station. The East Concourse features two 'Digital Video Display Walls' incorporating large-scale rear-projection and multi-screen displays presenting video art, news, weather, and cultural event listings. The interior of the building contains 2.29 square feet of rentable space, 32 high-speed elevators, and more than 8,000 tons of turbine-driven air-conditioning. The truck dock is located three stories below grade and is serviced by two heavy-duty hydraulic truck lifts.

The tenant space is virtually column-free, allowing for an open plan design for each tenant and design flexibility. In order to better serve its multiple tenants, current tower owner Mitsui Fudosan, (New York) Inc., completed a multi-million capital improvement program for its flagship property.

1251 Avenue of the Americas

(Formerly: Exxon Building)

Location: New York, New York, USA
Completion: 1972
Height: 750ft (228.6m)
Stories: 54
Area: 2.92 million ft²
Structure: Steel
Cladding: Bronze tinted aluminum, glass
Use: Office

2

1 View of building (Opposite)
2 Lobby art glass
3 North lobby/concierge desk
4 Elegant lobby details
5 Site plan
Photography: Peter Loppacher courtesy Mitsui Fudosan (1);
Fred Georges courtesy Mitsui Fudosan (3);
courtesy Mitsui Fudosan (2,4)

3

4

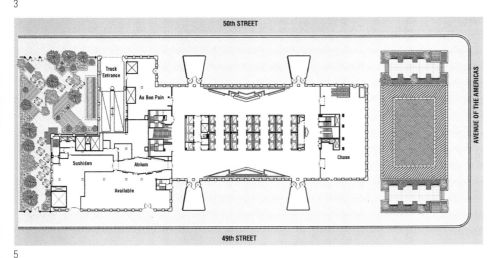

5

Architect: Harrison, Abramovitz & Harris
Structural Engineer: Edwards & Hjorth
Services Engineer: Syska & Hennesy
Developer: Rockefeller Center Inc. and Standard
    Oil Company of New Jersey
General Contractor: George A. Fuller Construction Co.

One Penn Plaza, at 57 stories, soars above midtown Manhattan's Central Business District. The tower is located at one of New York's most vibrant nodes of transportation, commercial, and entertainment activity. When first conceived in the 'Soaring Sixties,' the United States economy was expanding and this block of Manhattan's west side was considered an ideal location.

Positioned between 33rd and 34th Streets, 7th and 8th Avenue, the building derives its name from the old Pennsylvania Station which was demolished in 1966. The tower is a part of a larger complex including Two Penn Plaza, Madison Square Garden, the underground railway station, and a retail commercial concourse.

Elevators and escalators from the building's lobby lead directly into Pennsylvania Station providing links to four major city subway lines; the PATH system, the Long Island Railroad, New Jersey Transit and Amtrak service. One Penn Plaza also has a garage for 695 cars.

Since solid rock was close to the surface, excavation of the three levels below ground— another 17 feet below the Long Island Railroad concourse—represented one of the largest rock excavation jobs in New York construction history. Construction had to be scheduled so as to permit continuous operation of the Long Island and Pennsylvania train terminals.

The slim steel and glass tower is sheathed in gray heat-and-glare-resistant glass, accented by vertical mullions of anodized aluminum. The tower is buttressed by two lower portions 7 and 11 stories high. The bottom of the pedestal that frames the tower extends the entire width of the block on the 7th Avenue side. To the west the complex faces a landscaped plaza more than an acre in size. Stores and banks occupy the east and west sides of the plaza.

The architects slightly indented the four corners of the tower, thus gaining some extra corner offices. By locating the mechanical rooms on the 12th and 13th floors rather than at the top, contractors installing the refrigeration equipment, the piping, plumbing, and sheet metal during construction were able to begin work without waiting for the structural steel framework to be completed. This saved six to nine months in completion of the building, resulting in earlier occupancy.

One Penn Plaza

Location: New York, New York, USA
Completion: 1972
Height: 750ft (228.6m)
Stories: 57
Area: 2.4 million ft²
Structure: Steel
Cladding: Glass curtain wall
Use: Office

2

3

4

1 One Penn Plaza (Opposite)
2 View from ground level
3 Entrance
4 Street level view
Photography: courtesy Helmsley-Spear (1,2);
Douglas Mason (3,4)

Architect: Kahn & Jacobs
Structural Engineer: The Office of James Ruderman
Services Engineer: Jaros, Baum & Bolles
Developer: Mid City Associates (Harry Helmsley)
General Contractor: Morse Diesel
   Construction Co.

Situated on 26 acres of Boston's Back Bay section is Prudential Tower, Boston's first mixed-use development. It is built on a raised plaza that takes up a large portion of the site. With a daily population of 30,000 persons, the multi-level complex was carefully planned to separate pedestrian and vehicular traffic by utilizing air-rights over the six-lane Massachusetts Turnpike and two tracks of the Boston and Albany Railroad. The master plan was conceived to meet objectives of long-range phased construction while providing for the wide variety and diverse needs of major office occupants, residents, hotel guests, shoppers, and tourists.

The 52-story Prudential Tower rises 750 feet above ground level and contains 1.2 million square feet of usable space. The interior boasts an updated marble lobby which provides access to the center core of elevators.

The building is sheathed in gray and green structural glass. The 8,100 fixed-glass windows are set into a nine-and-a-half-inch-deep aluminum grillwork. The windows are grouped in pairs and separated by two-foot-wide opaque colored glass panels.

The 50th-floor skywalk observation deck provides visitors with a splendid view of much of Boston. The Tower also contains a gourmet restaurant, Top of the Hub, enclosed by glass walls.

Three 27-story, steel-framed apartment buildings occupy the northeast portion of the Prudential Center site and a 25-story office building faces south. Other buildings on the 26-acre site provide facilities for a variety of specialty shops and retail stores. Landscaping includes a large terraced plaza, 210 x 210 feet, and a smaller one to the north which provides outdoor seating for a food court. Access to all buildings is through glass-enclosed pedestrian retail arcades with direct escalator access from street level. Boston's largest hotel and its only convention center are connected to the site.

The Prudential Tower is supported by 144 steel-encased concrete and steel caissons that extend an average of 150 feet to bedrock. A special 'floating' foundation has been constructed for the balance of the area.

The Prudential Tower and its surrounding complex fulfilled Boston's goal of creating a more pedestrian-friendly interaction between the South End, the Back Bay and the city as a whole.

Prudential Tower

Location: Boston, Massachusetts, USA
Completion: 1964
Height: 750ft (228.6m)
Stories: 52
Area: 1.5 million ft²
Structure: Steel
Cladding: Glass
Use: Office

2

3

4

5

1 Prudential Tower and reflecting pool (Opposite)
2 Conference room
3 Redevelopment '94 Tower lobby
4 Office
5 Boylston entrance
Photography: courtesy The Luckman Partnership (1);
William Huber (2,3,4,5)

**Architect: The Luckman Partnership with Hoyle,
  Doran & Berry**
Structural Engineer: Edwards & Hjorth
Services Engineer: Syska & Hennessy
Developer: Prudential Insurance Company

Two California Plaza is one element in an eleven and a half-acre mixed-use complex in downtown Los Angeles along Bunker Hall. The complex includes three towers, of which Two California Plaza, the second to be built, is the tallest. The complex also features museums, theaters, dance studios, condominiums, retail spaces, and parking. A public fountain next to the building can be turned into a performance space.

With a form similar to One California Plaza, built earlier, Two California Plaza is 10 stories taller and has two notches at the corners, unlike the smaller tower which has but one. Along with the expanded possibilities for corner offices, the additional notch provides the opportunity to carry this form around the top of the building, giving it a unique 'cap' crowned by the striking band of light that was introduced to the Los Angeles skyline by One California Plaza.

Both towers feature two curving corners opposite one another and both are sheathed in Brazilian Sanduba granite at the base. A glass curtain wall forms the skin of the towers. The skin is comprised of three shades of reflective glass set in anodized aluminum and stainless steel mullions. This surface creates an intriguing interplay of reflections, not only between the building and its surrounding environment, but also with One California Plaza, as they reflect each other. The base is punctured with distinctive square and round windows.

The structural system, consisting of ductile moment-resisting steel frames forming a framed tube, was designed to resist seismic lateral loads and wind. The concrete structure below the tower consists of waffle slabs, reinforced concrete columns and sheer walls. Spread footings were utilized for the entire project except for the plaza level portion over Olive Street, which is supported by drilled, poured-in-place belled caissons.

Two California Plaza

Location: Los Angeles, California, USA
Completion: 1992
Height: 750ft (228.6m)
Stories: 52
Area: 1.27 million ft²
Structure: Steel
Cladding: Glass
Use: Office

3

1 Two California Plaza (Opposite)
2 View of notched corner
3 Artists rendering of Watercourt at California Plaza
Photography: courtesy John A. Martin & Associates

2

Architect: Arthur Erickson Associates
Associate Architect: A.C. Martin & Associates
Structural Engineer: John A. Martin & Associates
Services Engineer: Hayakawa & Associates
Developer: Bunker Hill Associates

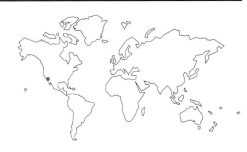

It has been said that what makes a tall building tall, is structure. Different designers have different responses to this question of how to support a tall building, and these different responses determine the forms these buildings take. In the 1980s the prototypical skyscraper was sought using a tube-in-tube structure. Later a revolutionary triangular framing system was developed in which concrete and steel were used, such as in the construction of the Bank of China. In all of these buildings structure not only held up the building but also determined its exterior, literally so in the Bank of China.

The MLC Centre tower is supported by eight massive columns that change in plan shape and area as they rise in relation to the different loads they must support. The columns are located to avoid the two underground railway tunnels which cross the site diagonally. The number and location of the columns was the essential determinant for the form of the tower. Between these columns are custom-designed, structurally expressive, long-span I-shaped facade beams. In between these beams are the ribbon windows of each floor, which are recessed for protection from the sun. For aesthetics and durability, all of the exterior structure is faced with a white quartz finish. The combination of these elements resulted in what has been called a 'venetian blind effect.'

The MLC Centre is technically a tube-in-tube type concrete tower. Combined with the exterior structure is a rigid load-bearing core. The beam structure which supports each floor also acts as connection between the core and exterior elements. On the first floor, because of the need for a raised ceiling in the lobby, this connection differs and is compensated for by a specially designed heavy floor, which is exposed structurally on the lobby ceiling.

The Centre is part of a complex which also contains restaurants, shops, cinemas, an open plaza, and the Royal Theatre. The tower occupies the southern portion of the site, thus allowing the other activities on the site to be on the sun-facing, northern side. The complex features the works of a variety of modern artists including Alexander Calder and Josef Albers.

MLC Centre

Location: Sydney, Australia
Completion: 1978
Height: 751ft (229m)
Stories: 65
Area: 1.2 million ft^2
Structure: Concrete
Cladding: White quartz
Use: Office

2

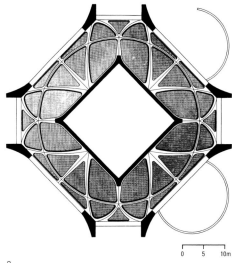

3

5

1 MLC Centre with Sydney Harbour in the
   background (Opposite)
2 Construction begins
3 Reflected ceiling plan of entrance level structures
4 Looking up, with 'half mushroom' projecting plaza alcove
5 Theatre Royal lobby
Photography: Max Dupain courtesy Harry Seidler & Associates
(1,2,4,5)

4

Architect: Harry Seidler & Associates
Structural Engineers: Civil & Civic Pty Ltd, Lehmann
   & Talty Pty, DT Broughton & Associates
Structural Consultant: Studio Nervi
Mechanical Engineer: Environ Mechanical
   Services Pty
Electrical Engineer: Civil & Civic Pty Ltd

Developer: The Mutual Life & Citizens Assurance Co.
General Contractor: Civil & Civic Pty Ltd

Serving as the headquarters for Equitable Life, just west of the former Equitable building on Sixth Avenue, this 51-story building rises above its surroundings with sweeping views of both the east and west sides of midtown Manhattan.

Completed in 1986 and containing 1.6 million square feet of rentable space, this was the first major structure on Seventh Avenue built in accordance with New York City's revised zoning ordinance, which sought to encourage development on the west side.

The structure has setbacks which bring light to the narrow 51st and 52nd Streets. These setbacks in the facade are boldly articulated with two-story deep recesses. At the top of the building are executive common rooms which display Equitable's art collection. Facing east and west are two vaulted spaces with large arched windows, lit at night, contributing further to the magic of the New York skyline.

The amenities at street level include a five-story skylight atrium on Seventh Avenue, two art galleries operated by the Whitney Museum, a grand hallway running from Sixth to Seventh Avenue connecting Equitable's new and old headquarters, a seven-story skylit galleria connecting 51st and 52nd Streets, public plazas, and an escalator to a lower concourse level with connections to Rockefeller Center and the subway system. A five-story atrium displays additional artwork, including a 32-x 64-foot mural. A through-block galleria displays murals on its exterior walls. Bronze sculptures flank the escalators connecting the concourse level below with its health club, swimming pool, 500-seat auditorium, and an underground pedestrian way to Rockefeller Center.

The steel structure, which is clad in Indiana limestone and Brazilian granite, utilizes a modified system of two-story trusses (outrigger type) at the 11th and 36th floors. These act as column transfers at the building setbacks. They also take wind loads, engaging all the columns across the building. Belt trusses connect to the outrigger trusses and assist in distribution of wind shear. Finally 'hat' trusses are used at the top of the structure. Taking advantage of their structural form, it was a convenient place to accommodate the mechanical equipment and elevator machine rooms.

Equitable Tower

Location: New York, New York, USA
Completion: 1986
Height: 752ft (229.2m)
Stories: 51
Area: 1.6 million ft²
Structure: Steel
Cladding: Indiana limestone, Brazilian granite
Use: Office

2

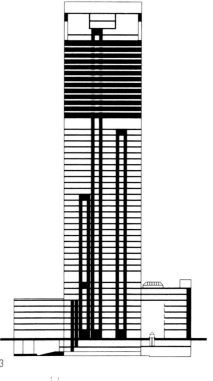

3

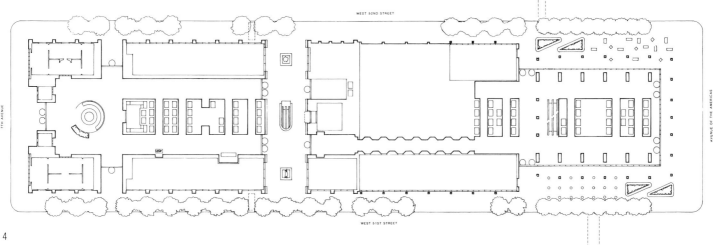

4

5

6

1 Equitable Tower (Opposite)
2 Cutaway view of basement
3 Elevation
4 Site plan
5 Under construction
6 View of lobby

Photography: Mark Ivins courtesy John M.Y. Lee/Michael Timchula Architects (1,6); Chris Minerva/Tamin Productions Inc. courtesy John M.Y. Lee/Michael Timchula Architects (5)

Architects: Edward Larrabee Barnes and Associates with John M.Y. Lee, Architects
Structural Engineer: Weiskopf & Pickworth
Services Engineer: Cosentini Associates
Developer: The Equitable Life Assurance Society of the US
General Contractor: Turner Construction Company Inc.

Three First National Plaza complex occupies a prime location near the financial center and downtown commercial district of Chicago's Loop. The project consists of a 57-story tower, an 11-story building which houses a private club, and a central 9-story glazed public lobby. At ground level, the complex connects with the Loop's system of all-weather pedestrian passages, with all the connections converging on the atrium lobby. The tower shape, with its sawtooth geometry, provides multiple corner offices while retaining a degree of openness along busy Madison Avenue. At the top six levels, stepped greenhouse offices provide panoramic views of the city and Lake Michigan.

The low-rise section has larger floor areas and maintains a height compatible with its neighbors to the north. The foundations of the building are reinforced concrete caissons to bedrock for the tower and to hard pan for the low-rise portion. The structural system combines steel and reinforced concrete allowing column-free interior space. The cladding uses cold spring Carnelian granite, making it one of the few all-granite buildings in the city.

Bronze reflective glass is also employed on the exterior, with aluminum mullions and warm gray spandrel panels. Bay windows, a traditional element of Chicago's turn-of-the-century architecture, are a central feature of the tower, designed to provide light and views to its tenants within this tight urban setting. These bay windows can be found in landmark Chicago buildings such as the Rookery, Monadnock, and Manhattan and Chicago Stock Exchange.

Office areas and mezzanine balconies look into the sloping atrium serving as a public space sheathed in clear and bronze-tinted glass and containing a variety of retail shops and restaurants.

The developer felt that a prestigious office building must have an impressive presence, luxurious and appealing spaces, and a dramatic entrance. People come into direct physical and visual contact with these tactile elements—and thus high priority was allotted to high-quality materials in the atrium lobby and on the exterior and interior of the building. Sumptuous bronze and leather finishes adorn the elevators. Furthermore, the entire project is completely accessible to the handicapped (it was the first office building to be designed in compliance with the new Illinois accessibility standards). The project also incorporated a number of innovative design features to maximize energy conservation, such as a dual-pane window system that reduces energy transfer across the glass, minimizing the expense of heating and air-conditioning.

Three First National Plaza

Location: Chicago, Illinois, USA
Completion: 1981
Height: 753ft (229.5m)
Stories: 57
Area: 1.5 million ft²
Structure: Mixed
Cladding: Bronze reflective glass
Use: Office

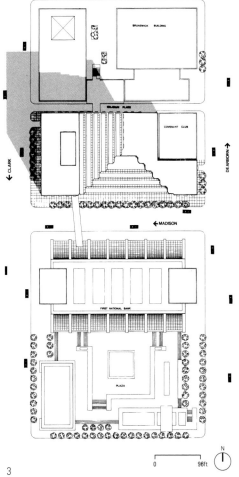

1 Three First National Plaza in the Chicago skyline (Opposite)
2 Atrium entrance
3 Site plan
4 View from street level
Photography: Hedrich-Blessing courtesy Skidmore, Owings
& Merrill

Architect: Skidmore, Owings & Merrill (SOM)
Landscape Architect: SOM
Structural Engineer: SOM
Services Engineer: I.A. Naman & Associates, Inc.
Owner/Developer: Gerald D. Hines Interests
General Contractor: Turner Construction Company

This slender 60-story Tower is the result of an ingenious transfer of unused air-rights over the Music Hall, now protected as a landmark structure. Squeezed between the seven-story landmark Carnegie Hall and five-story Russian Tea Room, the Tower's 57th Street elevation is only 50 feet wide. Using modern construction methods and means of architectural expression, the new Tower is designed to be a harmonious addition to a larger family of masses, extending the architecture of the hall and reinterpreting its system of ornament.

The six-story height of the Tower's base is determined by the cornice line of the Music Hall. Above this level, the Tower is set back to respect Carnegie Hall's 'Campanile'-like studio addition, with its large overhanging cornice. Essentially the building consists of two interlocking slabs, one tall and one small, engineered as a 'double-tube' with the wind-resisting elements incorporated directly into the poured-in-place walls. This type of structure, with closely spaced columns, was the most efficient design available.

Like Carnegie Hall, the exterior skin is primarily brick. The basic color was chosen to complement Carnegie Hall through the use of three compatible shades that create a pattern. Window sills, lintels, and accents are precast concrete, tinted to recall the terracotta decoration of the historic landmark and its honey-colored Roman brick.

The base is elegant in granite and stone details, which blend gracefully into Carnegie Hall without imitating it. The Tower's facades recall those of the Music Hall, its major components bound together by wide colored bands at six-story intervals, similar to the 100-year-old landmark building's cornice.

The Tower's top is a dark green glazed brick frieze beneath an open metalwork cornice, recalling the attic story of the Hall but proportionate to the height of the Tower. "The irony of Carnegie Hall Tower, which bears the name of a man who built his fortune in steel," wrote Michael Crosbie in *Architecture Magazine*, "is its concrete structure."

The structural engineers concluded that the building's sway from wind forces would in fact be reduced with concrete, since the cycle of motion due to wind loads is longer than that of a steel building (because of its greater weight), and this longer period reduces the acceleration and thus decreases the sensation of sway that might be felt by the occupants. Should the need arise, however, the engineers left room at the building's top for a damping mechanism.

Carnegie Hall Tower

Location: New York, New York, USA
Completion: 1991
Height: 757ft (230.7m)
Stories: 60
Area: 530,000 ft²
Structure: Concrete
Cladding: Roman brick, granite, stone
Use: Office

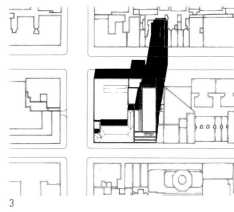

3

4

2   5

1   View of tower (Opposite)
2   Detail of overhanging cornice
3   Site plan
4   Music Hall
5   Interior of elevator
Photography: Jeff Goldberg/Esto courtesy Cesar Pelli & Associates (1,2,4,5)

Architect: Cesar Pelli & Associates
Associate Architect: Brennan Beer Gorman/
**   Architects, P.C.**
Structural Engineer: Robert Rosenwasser
**   Associates, P.C.**
Services Engineer: Cosentini Associates
Developer: Rockrose Development Corporation
Construction Manager: HRH Construction Company

The skyline of the quaint colonial tourist town of George Town, Penang, Malaysia, is dominated by the circular tower of the Kompleks Tun Abdul Razak (KOMTAR) Building. At the time of its construction, the complex was the largest urban redevelopment project undertaken by the Malaysian Government. It was designed to meet the growing demand for civic, administrative, commercial, and housing space in the city. KOMTAR also serves as a symbol of order and stability for the town and the province. Although the goal of the project was to preserve the historic character of the town, its modern form stands in stark contrast to the smaller buildings around it.

Strategically located in the heart of the business district, the four-story KOMTAR podium occupies an 11-hectare site. The tower itself serves as the government center for the region. Government offices, which were spread throughout the city, were relocated to the tower to provide more effective services. The circular tower rests upon this podium, one of many elements in the complex. The podium includes shopping, residences, and office spaces, a hawker's center, cinemas, a bus terminal, post office, fire station, conference center, public display area, health clinic, police post, swimming pool, garage, pedestrian mall, and a multi-purpose hall (enclosed by a glass geodesic dome).

The circular tower is actually a 12-sided geometric block, which rests upon foundations which vary between seven and nine feet thick. It is designed to withstand wind and earthquake loadings equivalent to four on the Richter scale. The interior organization is expressed on the exterior with concrete bands signifying mechanical floors which divide the building into three zones. The two penthouse floors are recessed, creating a dark shadow around the top of the building. The roof supports mechanical equipment and a helipad.

Kompleks Tun Abdul Razak Building

Location: George Town, Penang, Malaysia
Completion: 1985
Height: 760ft (231.7m)
Stories: 65
Area: 765,000 ft²
Structure: Concrete
Cladding: Concrete
Use: Office

2

3

5

1 Night view KOMTAR Building (Opposite)
2 Top of KOMTAR with microwave installation and helipad
3 KOMTAR Building stands tall in the George Town skyline
4 Ground floor plan
5 Podium of KOMTAR and Penang Road entrance
6 Cascading stairway leading to tower
Photography: OBK courtesy Heritage Research Sdn Bhd (1,3,5); Vince Yeap courtesy
Heritage Research Sdn Bhd (2); JBIS courtesy Heritage Research Sdn Bhd (6)

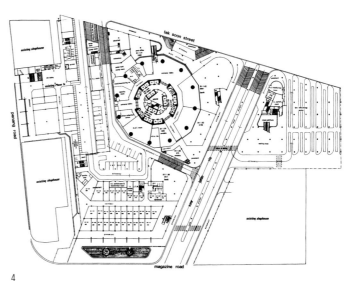

4

6

Architect: Jurubena Bertiga International Sdn
Structural Engineers: Ove Arup Partnership, Arup
   Jururunding Sdn Bhd
Services Engineer: Juiaraconsult Sdn Bhd
Developer: Penang Development Corporation
Contractors: Oh Teck Thye (Pte) Ltd (foundation);
   Lim Kah Ngam Sdn Bhd (superstructure)

Built in the southwest corner of the Shinjuku New Center area, this complex of offices, hotel, and showrooms serves as the terminus of an axis created by the long, narrow Chuo Public Park running north–south. This axis determined the building's orientation and the characteristic configuration of Tokyo's skyline. This multi-purpose building complex with its high-rise tower also can be seen as an extension of Chuo Park, with a large portion of the site carefully landscaped. An atrium inside further enhances the lush green atmosphere.

This building, rising to a height of 764 feet, consists of 52 floors above ground and 5 floors below. The overall great mass of the building has been articulated as a configuration of three diminishing towers to minimize its impact on the surrounding area and reduce the shadow over the park. It also made a gesture to preserve the continuity with the surrounding business district by matching the orientation of the city hall complex nearby.

This mixed-use building encloses 2.84 million square feet and accommodates a luxury hotel with 178 rooms. Arriving guests are greeted with a breathtaking view of the city as they ride the shuttle elevator connecting the hotel's second floor entrance hall with the 41st floor sky lobby. The view from the top floor hotel rooms is equally spectacular.

Below the hotel are 30 floors of office space. With its 2.7-meter-high ceilings and a raised access panel floor system, an unconstrained working space was created which would be very responsive to various needs of the tenants. The lower levels of the building contain a series of showrooms known as the 'Ozone,' serving as a multi-purpose design center.

Tokyo Gas Shinjuku District Heating and Cooling Center maintains a heating and cooling plant on the basement level, and showrooms on the first and second levels. The atrium connects the various parts of the building to the Shinjuku Central Heating Station.

Shinjuku Park Tower

Location: Tokyo, Japan
Completion: 1994
Height: 764ft (232.9m)
Stories: 52
Area: 2.8 million ft²
Structure: Steel
Cladding: Precast concrete panels, granite
Use: Multiple

2

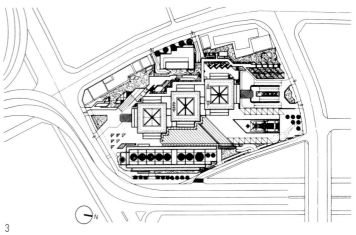

3

4

1 Appearing like three distinct towers, Shinjuku Park Tower
   is actually one (Opposite)
2 Shinjuku Park Tower detail
3 Site plan
4 Atrium
Photography: Osamu Murai courtesy Kenzo Tange Associates

Architect: Kenzo Tange Associates
Structural Engineer: Kobori Research Complex, Inc.
Services Engineer: Inuzuka Engineering Consultants
Developer: Tokyo Gas Urban Project

This building's basic form was shaped by the site which is just north of the Ritz-Carlton Hotel, linking Peachtree Street and Peachtree Center Avenue. Within this centrally located site, a twin tower 770 feet tall soars toward the sky.

The building was designed to create a visual impression of two towers, square in shape, joined together at the middle by a recessed plan culminating in classically inspired twin temples seven stories tall, acting visually as elegant crowns.

The base of the twin towers has a seven-story 60-foot-tall skylit atrium, 100 square feet in plan. The atrium features granite finishes and archways, which are covered in glass and let in daylight through an ornamental grillwork. Bold geometric patterns of granite paving also run throughout the atrium and elevator lobby spaces. The elevator lobby features a 30-foot barrel-vaulted ceiling and five elevator banks with 25-passenger and two service elevators.

In addition, approximately 15,000 square feet of retail space are accommodated by the atrium and lobby, imparting vitality to this light-filled space and inviting pedestrian activity.

Within the three-block radius, multiple business and shopping activities are to be found, including a wide variety of restaurants and clubs. One-half-block away, the MARTA stations are located, connecting the building to Atlanta's Hartsfield International Airport. From the main lobby and elevators there is a direct connection to the parking garage.

At the typical floors of the Towers, slender shafts of granite and gray tinted glass run the full height of the building with their corners deeply notched further enhancing the verticality of the Towers. These typical floors of the Tower offer a highly efficient rentable space with up to 12 corner offices per floor.

From east and west, the Tower appears as a single shaft of granite; from the north and south, as a twin tower form connected even as a single building.

191 Peachtree Tower was expressly designed to enhance the image and vitality of downtown Atlanta, both at street level and against the sky. The Tower reinforces the continued and growing confidence of the future of downtown Atlanta— a vital and international city.

191 Peachtree Tower

Location: Atlanta, Georgia, USA
Completion: 1991
Height: 770ft (234.7m)
Stories: 50
Area: 1.2 million ft²
Structure: Mixed
Cladding: Granite, glass
Use: Multiple

2

3

4

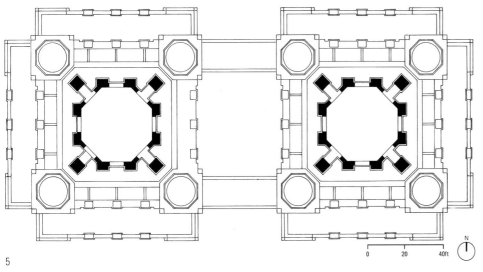

5

1   191 Peachtree Tower (Opposite)
2   Lobby
3   Sketch of lobby interior and roof
4   View of Atlanta skyline
5   Plan of top of building
Photography: Hedrich-Blessing courtesy Philip Johnson
Architects (1,2)

0   20   40ft

**Architects: John Burgee Architects with Raj Ahuja
and Philip Johnson Architects**
Associate Architect: Kendall/Heaton Associates, Inc.
Structural Engineer: CBM Engineers Inc.
Services Engineer: I.A. Naman and Associates, Inc.
**Developers: Cousins Properties, Inc., Dutch Institutional
Holding Co., and Gerald D. Hines Interests**
**General Contractor: Beers and Russell/Holder,
a joint venture**

Designed with the sun-drenched climate of Singapore in mind, the 52-story Treasury Building provided a new image and office space for government departments and commercial organizations. The striking cylindrical building, located in the heart of Singapore's business district, minimizes the exposed surface area, which reduces energy consumption.

The 1.4 million-square-foot building provides office space, retail shops, restaurants, public lobbies, and an underground parking garage. The tower stands 770 feet (235m) tall, and is clad with painted aluminum panels to reflect the sun. Bronze-tinted insulating glass helps keep the interior cool.

The building is notched on both the north and south facades to give the cylindrical form a sense of orientation. It also integrates the lower plan configuration with that of the site development at ground level. Emphasizing the tower's verticality, the notches suggest two adjoining semi-circular forms. One rises the full height of the structure from a two-story stepped-back podium. The other is foreshortened and cantilevered at the fifth level and is also four stories shy of the apex.

Under this cantilevered semi-circle is a triangular space-frame canopy. This entrance canopy provides protection from the weather at the ground level and lower-level entrances. The site is bisected diagonally to provide pedestrian access to the concourse from three corners. Sculpted openings in the paved surfaces of the concourse reveal a sunken retail plaza. Trees rising from the islands of ground cover, shrubbery echoing the surrounding landscape, and the spray of fountain jets penetrate from the lower plaza through the openings.

Escalators and stairs lead to the retail spaces and cafeteria on the lower level. The courtyard also provides pedestrian and vehicle access to the VIP entrance and lower elevator lobby. Underground pedestrian connections to adjacent buildings and to a mass transit station are located at this level.

The floor system is cantilevered 38 feet from a cast-in-place concrete core, and is supported by radial steel trusses. This system allows wind and gravity loads to be transferred to the core, leaving the interior free of columns. The enclosed radial girders provide coffers to accommodate lighting. The aluminum curtain wall minimizes the external wall load, and provides a surface resistant to salt air corrosion and pollution.

The Treasury Building hints of the elegance and technology of the future, while becoming a focal point of the urbanscape today. Its climate-sensitive design surpassed Singapore's codes for energy efficiency. Its entrance canopy, with Dakota mahogany flame-finish granite paving, pink borders, and red curbs, gives a sense of elegance to the 'front porch' of the streetscape of the city.

Treasury Building

Location: Singapore
Completion: 1986
Height: 770ft (234.7m)
Stories: 52
Area: 1.4 million ft²
Structure: Mixed
Cladding: Aluminium painted panels and bronze-tinted glass
Use: Multiple

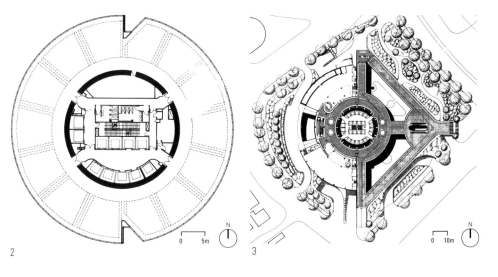

2

3

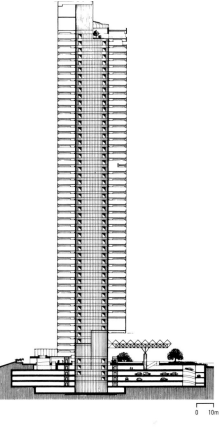

4

6

5

1 Singapore's Treasury Building, which was featured on the
   Singapore $50 banknote commemorating the 25th
   anniversary of the independence of Singapore (Opposite)
2 Typical floor plan, high rise
3 Site plan
4 Building section
5 Entrance canopy in the evening
6 Entrance canopy from inside
Photography: Peter Aaron/Esto courtesy The Stubbins
Associates (5,6)

Architect: The Stubbins Associates with Architects 61
Structural Engineers: Le Messurier Consultants with
  Ove Arup and Partners
Services Engineer: Ewbanks Preece Partnership
Developer: Singapore Treasury Building (Pte) Ltd

A 'not-entirely-happy circumstance' led to the development of the Norwest Tower in Minneapolis, Minnesota. When the original bank's headquarters burned down in 1982, the Norwest Corporation began to plan a large-scale project that would cover the entire block, including the half that the old Norwest Bank occupied. The preliminary design was scrapped however, when the partners could not agree. When the communications broke down, the Bank's representatives went ahead with the construction on their half of the site. The 'new' narrower rectangular dimensions led to an impressive and interesting solution.

The design was the architect's attempt at a Romantic approach to a Post-Modern skyscraper: to recreate the charisma and grandeur of the great skyscrapers of the 1920s and 1930s without the literal resurrection of those patterns. The resulting design "reflects the past but doesn't lie about the fact that it is new." The overall design can be visually traced to Raymond Hood's RCA Building in New York, a grand and sophisticated limestone tower.

Norwest Tower tapers slightly, rising gracefully from a solid, heavy granite base towards a lighter crown of glass and marble. The interior established a unique yet complementary identity: rather than compete with the grand shell, the designers opted for simple, classically modern materials and forms. The teller stations were represented in simple black and white shapes, alternating black granite walls with cleverly lit glass prisms. The interior was also detailed with medallions, chandeliers, and railings saved from the old original 16-story Northwestern National Bank Building. They, along with additional pieces, are featured in the grand rotunda and through-block lobby.

Most of the structure is clad in Minnesota stone, a golden-hue material also prevalent in many existing buildings downtown. Red Indian granite is used along the base of the building, complementing the limestone. White marble is also used for the vertically layered facade.

Norwest Tower is also as safe against fire as it is beautiful. Taking no chances after the Northwestern National Bank building burned, suffering nearly $100 million in damage in 1982, Norwest Corporation installed a $1.5 million sprinkler system, a smoke exhaust duct that runs the entire height of the building, pressurized stairwells, dedicated recall firefighter elevators, and a sophisticated fire command center.

Norwest Tower

Location: Minneapolis, Minnesota, USA
Completion: 1988
Height: 773ft (235.6m)
Stories: 57
Area: 2.02 million ft^2
Structure: Steel
Cladding: Red Indian granite, Minnesota stone, marble
Use: Office

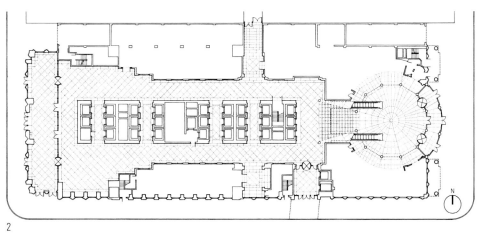

2

1 Norwest Tower (Opposite)
2 Typical first floor plan
3 Interior Bank lobby
4 View from the north
5 Building facade at street level
Photography: George Heinrich courtesy Cesar Pelli &
Associates (1,4); Balthazar and Christian Korab courtesy
Cesar Pelli & Associates (3,5)

4

3

5

Architect: Cesar Pelli & Associates
Associate Architect: Kendall/Heaton Associates
Interior Designer: STUDIOS Architecture
Structural Engineer: CBM Engineers
Services Engineer: I.A. Naman & Associates
Developers: Gerald D. Hines Interests and
   Norwest Bank

One Canada Square, better known as the former Canary Wharf Tower, at 774 feet, is the centerpiece of the entire Canary Wharf complex which also includes a shopping and cultural center and the Docklands Light Railway Station. Conceived under the Thatcher government, the project was to revitalize the Thames Dockland, but it soon became a very controversial project facing many difficulties, both economic and aesthetic.

This was the first skyscraper in London, which, according to its architect, tried to capture the essence of the skyscraper form and image and express it in a controlled and simple manner. One of 10 office buildings, the tower is a tall square prism with indented corners that culminates in a square-based pyramid.

The lobby connects adjacent water courts and promenades directly to the central concourse of the Retail and Assembly Building. These are clad in limestone and include shops, restaurants, and a central skylit multi-story public space with adjoining exhibition and meeting rooms.

The station for the Docklands Light Railway line is located at the second-floor level and is directly connected to the Tower through the concourse of the Retail Building. The station is the most important gateway for the entire project, which handles an average of 60,000 commuters each day.

The entire high-rise building, walls and pyramid roof, are clad in stainless steel. The ribs of the modular grid catch the light, creating a delicate tracery on the surface of the wall. The wall is articulated in a regular grid ten feet wide. In the center of each grid panel is a large window of clear, untinted glass. The metallic surface of the tower reflects the light and color of the sky as the weather, seasons, and time of day change.

Not only does the metallic surface of the Tower reflect the light and color, but soon after its completion it also blocked television reception to about 100,000 viewers and residents in northern London. The main difficulty was that this tallest and shiniest building reflected up to 80 percent of television reception—as compared to a more traditional building of brick or concrete, which reflects less than 5 percent of television signal's energy.

The engineers of BBC's main television station devised a solution, erecting a small transmission tower on a building near One Canada Square and supplied special antennas to the residents in the immediate area. However, those viewers further away to the north, due to Canary Wharf's reflections, received some signals a fraction of a second later 'conjuring up television ghosts.'

1

2

One Canada Square

(Formerly: Canary Wharf Tower)

Location: Isle of Dogs, London Borough, U.K.
Completion: 1991
Height: 774ft (235.9m)
Stories: 50
Area: 1.8 million ft²
Structure: Steel
Cladding: Stainless steel
Use: Office

3

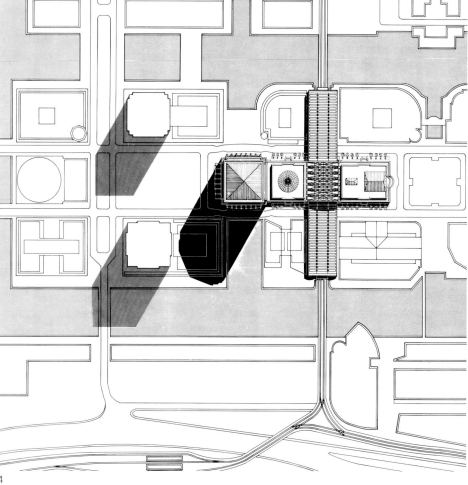

4

5

6

1   View from the Thames River (Opposite)
2&3 One Canada Square gleams in the sunlight
4   Site plan
5   Model shot
6   Exterior facade
Photography: Robert Bostwick courtesy Cesar Pelli & Associates
(1); Larry Ng courtesy Cesar Pelli & Associates (2,3,6);

Architect: Cesar Pelli & Associates
Associate Architect: Adamson Associates
Structural Engineers: M.S. Yolles & Partners in assocaiation with Frederick Gibberd Coombes & Partners
Services Engineer: The Mitchell Partnership (T.M.P.)
Electrical Engineer: H. H. Angus & Associates, Ltd

Developer: Olympia & York/LMI
General Contractor: Olympia & York/LMI

The redevelopment of a 1.6 acre site in the commercial district of downtown Minneapolis included the construction of First Bank Place at 58 stories tall and a 20-story building which provides transition to smaller, neighboring buildings and defines a park to the east. The complex, erected on an L-shaped plan, was designed by the architects to respond to three different urban conditions; nearby modern high-rises, low-rise historic neighbors, and a precious green park area in the otherwise congested central business district. On the corner, a glazed atrium linking the two components is set back to create an outdoor plaza which welcomes pedestrians entering the building. Inside is a conical rotunda, surrounded by restaurants and retail spaces. The architect unified these three distinct programs with related materials, simple forms, and a ground-level pedestrian arcade around the perimeter. On the second-level, the tower connects to adjacent blocks by two bridges.

The tower is formed by concentric arcs superimposed over a square. It is surmounted by a 45-foot-tall semi-circular steel crown with a 20-foot cantilever. While providing a distinctive image on the Minneapolis skyline, the crown also serves as a screen for cooling towers and antennae. Four composite supercolumns, which diminish in cross-sectional area as they rise, extend the full length of the building. Arranged in a cruciform pattern, these columns form a spine which supports the building. Moment-resisting frames along the perimeter help stabilize the columns. Three-story-deep Vierendeel girder bandages at three locations triple the tower's torsional stiffness and increase its lateral stiffness, while transferring gravity loads to the supercolumns and corner columns.

The structural system allows a column-free exterior facade. Above the 45th-floor, a nine-story-tall circular Vierendeel girder, which supports the floor loads, connects to the supercolumns, thus eliminating the need for additional columns from the floors below. Post-tensioned concrete floors in the basement create a three-story garage, also providing support for the building.

First Bank Place

Location: Minneapolis, Minnesota, USA
Completion: 1992
Height: 775ft (236.2m)
Stories: 58
Area: 1.5 million ft²
Structure: Mixed
Cladding: Granite
Use: Office

1 View of First Bank Place and park (Opposite)
2 Lit up at night
3 Glazed atrium
4 Intricate elevator doors
5 Rotunda
Photography: Christian Korab courtesy Pei Cobb Freed &
Partners (1,2); Philip Prowse courtesy Pei Cobb Freed &
Partners (3,4,5)

2

3

4

5

Architect: Pei Cobb Freed & Partners
Associate Architect: HKS, Inc.
Structural Engineer: CBM Engineers, Inc.
Mechanical Engineer: Cosentini Associates
Developer: IBM Associates Limited Partnership
General Contractor: Opus Corporation

The goal was to combine an office tower, hotel, shopping center, and plaza of high density in the very center of town, linking it with pedestrian bridges, parking garages, financial institutions, and department stores, around a central court over a full city block. The result was the 52-story IDS Center, with its beautiful Crystal Court.

The Investors Diversified Services (IDS) Center is the tallest building in the Minneapolis skyline. From the very beginning, it was applauded not only as a good building, but as one of the finest skyscraper groupings built in any American city within a decade, a complex that was fully respectful of the existing Minneapolis cityscape. The tower contains a 19-story hotel, an eight-story office building, and a two-story wing of shops, all located around a central glass-covered court, reaching 121 feet in height and stepping down as a pyramid of steel and glass. This Crystal Court is accessible on two different levels by eight entrances, two on every block, one above the other, allowing people to join in or to observe the crowds from above.

The building's main shaft is a 51-story, 775-foot-tall octagonal tower with eight small zig-zag setbacks along each of the four sides, creating 32 corner offices at each floor. These setbacks also act very effectively in visually reducing the overall bulk of the building, casting vertical shadows over the multi-faceted mirror-glass skin. The aesthetics of the skyscraper in relation to its urban environment was one of the major preoccupations of the architects, and one reason why they rejected the popular open plaza in favor of a climate controlled one, and also rejected the simple glass box in favor of a multi-faceted one.

The office tower has a two-story travertine marble-covered interior lobby. However the hotel has no real lobby, since the court accommodates most of the lobby functions (such as registration desk). The hotel rooms are staggered along a zig-zagged center corridor, giving most of the guests a corner window view.

Rather than the more common glass curtain wall modules of five-foot, the designer opted instead for two foot six inches. The result resembled a birdcage, further breaking the traditional box and giving it an elegant vertical emphasis. The eight-story office annex contains an underground parking garage which can accommodate 525 cars.

Every aspect of this full square block was developed for the convenience and enjoyment of the people, whether they be shoppers, visitors, tourists, tenants, or office employees. 'Getting around' and 'getting there' is what is most enjoyable.

IDS Center

Location: **Minneapolis, Minnesota, USA**
Completion: **1973**
Height: **775ft (236.2m)**
Stories: **52**
Area: **2.4 million ft²**
Structure: **Mixed**
Cladding: **Glass**
Use: **Multiple**

2

4

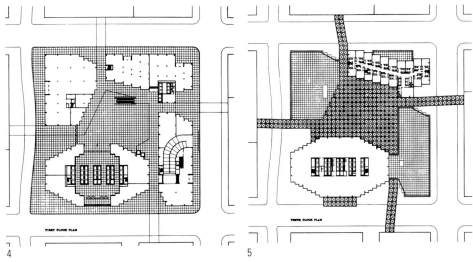

5

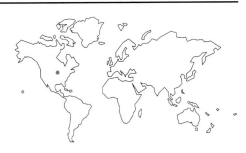

1 IDS Center (Opposite)
2 Crystal Court
3 IDS Center looking up from ground level
4 First floor plan
5 Tenth floor plan
Photography: Richard Payne courtesy Johnson/Burgee
Architects

3

Architects: John Burgee Architects and Philip
    Johnson Architects in association with
    Edward F. Baker
Landscape Architect: Zion & Breen
Structural Engineer: Severud-Perrone-Shurn-
    Conlin-Bandel

Services Engineer: Cosentini Associates
Electrical Engineer: Eitingon & Schlossberg
    Associates
Developer: Investors Diversified Services
General Contractor: Turner Construction Company
Interior Designer: John Burgee Architects and Philip
    Johnson Architects

During the optimistic era of the 1980s, many developers believed in boundless economic growth. So in 1985, plans were announced to build a mixed-use project for over $500 million. Worldwide Plaza was to occupy an entire city block (almost 4 acres), and include an office tower, housing, retail space, a parking garage, and a public plaza. The high-rise tower was planned for the eastern end of the block, and the apartment tower was to occupy the center of the site.

The developer chose a method known as the 'fast track.' In the interests of saving time and money, three activities would be allowed to overlap: financing, design, and construction. The building was to be built in a single phase where all the elements of the entire complex were designed to minimize disturbance since tenants would be moving in before completion. The developers projected that by the time the building was finished within two years, it would be two-thirds leased.

Worldwide Plaza can generally be divided into three parts: 1) the tall commercial tower on the east side, 47 stories high; 2) a 41-story residential tower, and 3) a 'u'-shaped pattern of townhouses enclosing a courtyard on the western part of the site. The entire complex steps down from high-rise (for commercial) to medium low-rise (for residential). The mid-block tower is reached directly from the public plaza, which is designed to promote pedestrian circulation. In addition there are pavilion entrances to six movie theaters below ground.

The office tower recalls the great New York skyscrapers of the past, but with greater width and mass. To make it more slender would have meant to make it more expensive, and the builders opted for squatness and speed.

With a glazed pyramidal top, the architect acknowledged the traditional shape of a skyscraper, which, like the classical column, divides the building into base, shaft, and capital. The base is granite, covered and enhanced by a soft elliptical curve containing exterior arcades. The shaft is simple, wide, and unadorned except for the slight tint of pink brick color. The roof—which modernist architects have neglected since World War II—has once again become fashionable.

Worldwide Plaza

Location: New York, New York, USA
Completion: 1989
Height: 778ft (237.1m)
Stories: 47
Area: 1.6 million ft² (office tower gross)
Structure: Steel
Cladding: Pink brick, granite
Use: Office

2

3

4

1 View of tower (Opposite)
2 Main entrance
3 Worldwide Plaza in the Manhattan skyline
4 Plaza and fountain
Photography: Jeff Goldberg/Esto Photographics courtesy
Skidmore, Owings & Merrill (1); Douglas Mason (2);
Ivan Zaknic (3,4)

Architect: Skidmore, Owings & Merrill (SOM)
   (office tower), Frank Williams & Associates
   (residential part)
Landscape Architect: THE SWA GROUP
Structural Engineer: SOM (office tower),
   R. Rosenwasser Associates (residential part)
Services Engineer: Cosentini Associates

Developers: ZCW Associates, The Zeckendorf
   Company, Worldwide Holdings Corporation,
   Arthur G. Cohen, K.G. Land New York Corporation
   (Kumagui Gami)
Construction Manager: H.R.H. Construction

This complex consists of a 52-story tower, a three-level pavilion with two-story galleries and a four-level base. The tower is placed at the southwest corner and the pavilion at the northeast corner of the site, leaving about 50 percent of the site free for a large plaza along California Street on the north side.

The level immediately below the plaza contains a pedestrian concourse with entrances from three streets. The concourse features a cafeteria and an auditorium with 220 seats, as well as many different shops. Below that level are truck delivery and pick-up facilities and a three-level basement garage for 420 cars.

The pavilion containing the main office branch of the bank is supported by four robust corner columns. The two gallery levels and the ground floor, accessible from Montgomery Street on the east side, offer a total floor area of 30,000 square feet.

The Bank of America Center tower covers an area 143 x 243 feet in plan, and contains a total floor area of 1.5 million square feet. The bank occupies about one-third of the office space, with the remainder made available for rental.

To highlight the sculptural quality of the 779-foot-high tower, a bay window design has been used. The upper floors are distinguished by irregular setbacks. A polished granite of reddish color, and bronze-tinted solar glass covers the steel frame of the Bank of America Center. Because of its location in old San Francisco, this textured granite was chosen over a glazed curtain wall facade.

On the standard floors, the windows point outwards and the columns are merged with the inside window posts, giving the appearance of a smooth skin which does not conceal the plastic shape of the building. However, the windows of the banking hall on the second and third floor point inwards so as to emphasize the columns and to preserve formal continuity with the recessed main lobby on the ground floor.

Built in 1969, Bank of America Center held the record for the tallest building in San Francisco for a scant three years until the Transamerica Pyramid was completed it in 1972.

Bank of America Center

Location: San Francisco, California, USA
Completion: 1969
Height: 779ft (237.4m)
Stories: 52
Area: 1.5 million ft²
Structure: Steel
Cladding: Reddish granite, bronze-tinted solar glass
Use: Office

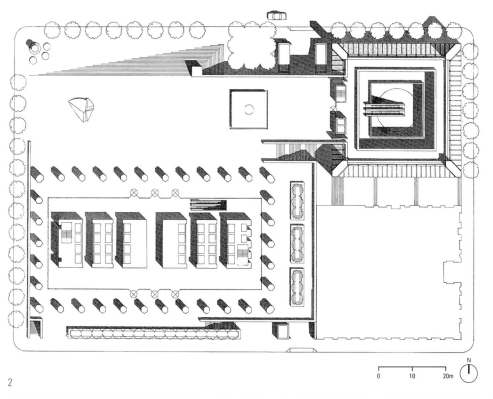

2

3

4

1 Bank of America Center was textured to blend with its
  lower neighbors (Opposite)
2 Site plan
3 Interior of pavilion
4 Jagged facade
Photography: Jerry Bragstad courtesy Skidmore, Owings
& Merrill (1,3); courtesy Bank of America World
Headquarters (4)

**Architects: Wurster Bernardi & Emmons, Inc./
  Skidmore, Owings & Merrill (SOM)
  (in joint venture)
Consulting Architect: Pietro Belluschi
Structural Engineer: H.J. Brunnier and Associates
Mechanical Engineer: SOM**

**Consulting Mechanical Engineer: William
  Di Giacomo & Associates
Electrical Engineer: SOM
Developer: Bank of America NT & SA
General Contractor: Dinwiddie - Fuller - Cahill,
  (in joint venture)**

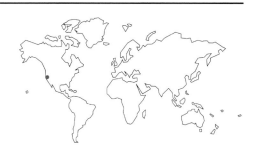

"It can appear alternately fanciful, energetic, and brooding—quite a range for a tall building in 1984. It could have been a little more than historicist veneer applied to another dumb box. Instead it reminds one of the days when skyscrapers were a big deal."

So said *Progressive Architecture* magazine about the NationsBank Center in Houston. This 56-story, 780-foot tower, originally designed for RepublicBank, was acquired by NCNB Texas in 1989. The 1.4 million square foot project, with its steep gable, reminiscent of Dutch guild halls and German municipal buildings, is another design which consciously tries to avoid any reference to modern architecture—including its neighbor, Penzoil Place, built by the same architects a decade earlier. Further, it borrows from the Gothic details of Renaissance palaces and the great galleries of the 19th century, embodying Romanticism and post-modernism.

It occupies a full block site in downtown Houston, except for one corner, which is occupied by the Western Union equipment building, and which proved too costly and complicated to relocate. Instead, it was decided that NationsBank Center would completely hide the Western Union switching station inside. It now stands completely independent of the skyscraper that covers it.

The plan approach was to divide the block, delineated by Smith and Louisiana Streets, Rusk and Capitol Avenues, into four quadrants. Along these cross axes, vaulted arcades run through the building, street to street. A grand banking hall is located in the quadrant adjacent to the switching station and extends above it. The major axis bisecting the block serves as an interior street, with four entrances. The arched entry to the banking hall is of monumental scale, rising 80 feet. This arch continues through the complex as an interior street, which is air-conditioned—a highly desirable feature in Houston during the summer months. The banking hall itself has a 120-foot ceiling which steps up symmetrically in layer upon layer of granite ribs, with the skylights above filling the hall with daylight.

The tower as well as the low building are sheathed in red granite and detailed in a similar pattern of rustication, with square inserts and four-pane widows up to the cornice line of the low building, while rising with its distinct shaft above. The shaft, alternating pilasters and mullions, create an A B A B A rhythm.

NationsBank Center

(Formerly: NCNB, and Republic Bank Center)

Location: Houston, Texas, USA
Completion: 1984
Height: 780ft (237.7m)
Stories: 56
Area: 1.4 million ft²
Structure: Steel
Cladding: Granite
Use: Office

2

3

4

5

6

1 NationsBank Center (Opposite)
2 12-story atrium banking hall and Western Union center
3 Rendering, NationsBank Center
4 Interior rendering
5 Interior 'street' entrance
6 Interior hall

Photography: Richard Payne courtesy John Burgee Architects
with Philip Johnson (1); Hedrich-Blessing courtesy
Ivan Zaknic (5); courtesy John Burgee Architects with
Philip Johnson (6)

Architect: Johnson/Burgee Architects
Structural Engineer: CBM Engineers
Services Engineer: I.A. Naman and Associates
Developer: Gerald D. Hines Interests

Once the largest stainless-steel-clad building in the world, Commerce Court West is just as remarkable on the inside as is the reflection it generates on the outside. Designed to complement the image of its 1929 Neo-Classical neighbor, the bank's original headquarters, Commerce Court West differs from its surroundings in subtlety of finish and simplicity in detailing.

The tower is the unabashed focus of a four-acre, four-building complex that defines an 80,000-square-foot public courtyard and surmounts an underground shopping concourse with pedestrian and subway links to similar complexes. The courtyard's centerpiece is a circular fountain surrounded by trees. The gray granite pavers of the courtyard extend into the lobbies of three new buildings.

Inside Commerce Court West, the perimeter walls are sheathed with the same stainless steel and glass as the exterior. The walls of the interior core are finished in gray granite to complement the stainless steel, whereas the ceiling is enclosed with aluminum panels. The upper portion of the banking hall has tall vertical windows, whereas the lower part features long horizontal strips. Teller counters were designed to contrast these finishes with a white marble top and polished stainless steel rails. The elevator doors feature an etched chevron of the bank's watermark. Escalators for the underground concourse penetrate through a circular opening defined by glass with polished stainless steel handrails. The 57th-floor features an observation deck.

The structure of the tower is expressed clearly on the outside skin. Reflective glass bands are flush with the unique pebble-finish 1/8-inch stainless steel cladding. It is U-shaped, with seams at the column center lines and at the top of the glass bands. The cladding is hung from the structure, allowing the frame and the skin to move independently from one another in expansion and contraction from the weather. All movement occurs at the column center lines, which are 57 feet apart. Erection of the 33,000 tons of structural steel took one year to complete.

The cladding itself acts as a rain screen and in combination with insulation and a vapor barrier creates a virtually airtight structure. The tower also features life-safety systems that were state-of-the-art at the time, with sprinklers, pressurized stairs and a smoke-exhaust system.

Commerce Court West

(Also known as: Canadian Imperial Bank of Commerce)

Location: Toronto, Canada
Completion: 1973
Height: 784ft (239m)
Stories: 57
Area: 1.46 million ft²
Structure: Mixed
Cladding: Stainless steel, glass
Use: Office

1 Commerce Court West (Opposite)
2 The sun glints off a shining facade
3 Public courtyard
4 Detail of entrance
5 Christmas lighting in courtyard
6 View at night
Photography: Balthazar Korab courtesy Pei Cobb Freed & Partners (1,6); Ezra Stoller-Esto courtesy Pei Cobb Freed & Partners (2,3); Ivan Zacnic (4,5)

2

3

4

5

6

Architect: I.M. Pei & Associates (now Pei Cobb
   Freed and Partners)
Associate Architect: Page & Steel
Structural Engineer: C.D. Carruthers & Wallace
   Consultants in association with Weiskopf &
   Pickworth
Mechanical Engineer: G. Granek & Associates
Electrical Engineer: Jack Chisvin & Associates

Owner/Developer: Canadian Imperial Bank
General Contractor: V. K. Mason-Peter Kiewit Sons
   Co. of Canada Ltd

As the new headquarters for the Mercantile National Bank at the time of its conception, the 787-foot Bank One Center, as it is now called, was not only innovative in its approach to design and construction, it was also a path-breaking concept in the field of banking. Providing a vast array of new financial and customer services, it became in effect a complete financial resource center in electronic banking, discount stock brokerage operations, investment advice, and other services.

The 60-story tower of granite and glass, formerly known as Momentum Place, fronts Ervay Street. At the base of the tower, set back from the street by a garden, the bank building has as its centerpiece, a major space housing the bank lobby in the form of a barrel-vault six levels high. Bridges to the tower lobby overlook the trading floor below, with traders on full display. Rising behind the bank is the office tower with its arched granite entrances on both Elm and Main Streets, and a fourth entrance through a landscaped area of St. Paul Street. The St. Paul Street side has an open plaza, richly landscaped with trees to provide a people-oriented environment at street level.

As the building rises, the setbacks topped with vaulted forms give the building a tapered appearance by emphasizing its vertical thrust. The top of the tower is crowned with a cross vault similar to the vaulted and skylit bank below, thus integrating the top and the base and giving the building its distinguished profile against the skyline.

The banking hall is sheathed in pink granite, and the tower lobby is lined in creamy Botticino marble with red Alicante marble trim and paved in an ornamental marble pattern of cream and black. The cross-vaulted roof is covered in copper.

The ceiling of the banking hall was a study in contrasts, requiring both electronic wizards and time-honored artisans working side by side: massive amounts of electrical and computer wiring inside the ceiling, and $7.5 million worth of beautiful cherry panelling and $5 million worth of marble hiding it all.

The tower's design echos classical architecture inside and out, in spite of its modern construction technology, intricate geometry, and unconventional structural frame. A mix of structural systems were utilized, thus complicating the construction sequence but saving a substantial amount of money. It was estimated that by using concrete sheer walls at the corners, with infills of composite columns and steel spandrels as well as composite steel and concrete beams on the floors, and all steel at the 50th-floor level where the tower changes from rectangular to cruciform shape, $2.4 million was saved over the cost of an all-steel structure.

Bank One Center

(Formerly: Momentum Place)

Location: Dallas, Texas, USA
Completion: 1987
Height: 787ft (239.9m)
Stories: 60
Area: 1.4 million ft²
Structure: Mixed
Cladding: Granite, glass
Use: Office

2

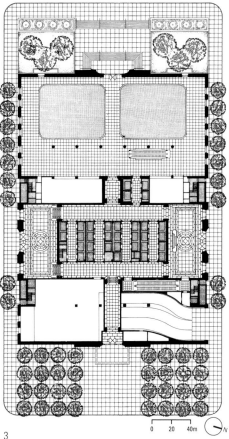

3

4

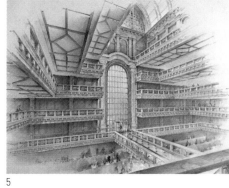

5

1 Bank One Center (Opposite)
2 Skyline of Dallas, with Bank One Center
3 Site plan
4 Bridges to the tower lobby overlook the trading floor below
5 Artist's rendering of lobby overlooking trading floor
Photography: Richard Payne courtesy Johnson/Burgee Architects

Architects: Johnson/Burgee Architects with Harwood K. Smith and Partners
Structural Engineer: The Datum/Moore Partnership
Services Engineers: Cosentini Associates/Steven Dunn & Partners
Developers: Cadillac Fairview Urban Developers and Mbank Dallas
Interior Designer: 3/D International

In the context of a group of significant and beloved landmark buildings, the John Hancock Tower slices through the historic fabric of old Boston. The building's presence on the skyline is more a sculpture than a building, while to the pedestrian, its massive presence defers to its decorative neighbors. Located on historic Copley Square, the Tower is placed next to the Boston Public Library, New Old South Church, and the Sheraton Copley Plaza Hotel. But its most important neighbor, Trinity Church, is so close as to be reflected in the mirrored glass of the Tower.

The introduction of this large office building into such a small-scaled precinct led the architect to adopt a minimalist scheme of steel and reflective glass to animate the plaza. By locating the Tower next to the church, the pedestrian perspective is steered toward the dominating image of the church, while the Tower becomes a by-product of the space. Placed on an angle to the church, the building creates a plaza which serves to highlight the church while doubling as an entrance to the Tower. The entrance to the Tower was originally demarcated by plastic bubbles, which have since been changed to a glass shed. On the other sides of the site, the first floors of the Tower fill the site and match the roof lines of the adjacent hotel. On the square, the Tower's rhomboid shape emphasizes the planar while diminishing the apparent mass of the structure. Notches cut into the end walls accentuate the verticality of the Tower.

Inside the lobby is a high-tech extravaganza of supergraphic arrows and numbers and curving mirror-finished railings and columns. Color-coded, doubledecker elevators and escalators transport users to their floors, whereas tourists take a separate elevator to the 60th-floor observation deck. Typical floors featured an office landscape furniture system, but problems with privacy and acoustics forced a change toward a more traditional office layout.

Although the finished product has become a landmark, the road to its completion was paved with potholes. During construction, the wooden pilings which support Trinity Church and the Sheraton Copley Plaza Hotel shifted, causing damage throughout the buildings when a retaining wall for the Tower failed. The John Hancock Tower owners paid for the repairs to the church and bought the hotel. Later the windows, constructed with double-layer mirror glass, began popping from their aluminum mullions during windstorms. The large panes had to be replaced with a traditional single-thickness glass. This problem gave both the architect and engineer pause to reflect on the structure's durability. After much speculation, several tons of steel struts were added to the structure. These problems resulted in the building opening years behind schedule and millions of dollars over budget.

John Hancock Tower

Location: Boston, Massachusetts, USA
Completion: 1976
Height: 788ft (240.2m)
Stories: 60
Area: 2.06 million ft^2
Structure: Steel
Cladding: Steel, reflective glass
Use: Office

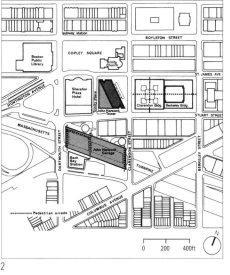

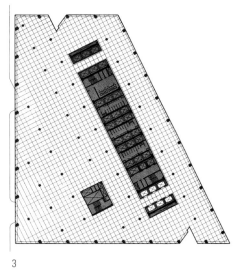

1 View of John Hancock Tower (Opposite)
2 Site plan
3 Typical floor plan
4 Skyline of Boston
5 Trinity church in front of John Hancock Tower
6 John hancock Tower reflects its surroundings
7 Entrance lobby
Photography: Gorchev and Gorchev courtesy Pei Cobb Freed
& Partners (1,5,6); Steve Rosenthal (4); Ivan Zaknic (7)

2

3

4

5

6

7

Architect: I.M. Pei & Partners
Structural Engineer: Office of James Ruderman
Services Engineer: Consentini Associates
Developer: Mutual Life Insurance Company

One of the early skyscrapers to exceed Philadelphia's previous 491 foot height limit, the designer of the Mellon Bank Center felt a 'special responsibility to create a dialogue with City Hall,' which was historically the tallest building in Philadelphia. This dialogue included the traditional tripartite design, with an oversized stone base, an aluminum and glass paneled shaft, and a lighted, pyramid structural top. Mellon Bank Center's dialogue with City Hall is more of a compliment than a discussion. Like City Hall, Mellon Bank Center is based upon a campanile style building. But while City Hall has a small tower attached to a large base, Mellon Bank Center has an oversized base upon which is centered the square shaft of the tower.

The neo-classicism of Mellon Bank is most obvious at the top of the tower, where the shaft terminates with an overhanging cornice. The cornice is accentuated by a number of architectural features, including stretching the glazing, which is lit at night to accent the impact of the overhang. This cornice not only terminates the shaft but also serves to separate the capital, accentuating the pyramidal framework. The pyramid was added purely for form.

Beyond its record breaking height of 792 feet, Mellon Bank Center also marked another first for Philadelphia: the use of a composite structure in a tall building in the city. While composite structures had been used in many other cities, Philadelphia was predominantly a steel town. To complicate matters, few laborers in the city had experience in this type of mixed construction.

Besides the coordination problem of concrete and steel, the site held several below-grade problems. The site is located above JFK Center, the major public transportation hub in center city. An underground street beneath the site had to be lowered a foot for the construction of Mellon Bank.

On street level, a winter garden was designed between Mellon Bank Center and its neighbor, Six Penn Center. The base of the building abuts JFK Boulevard, 18th Street, and Market Street, with retail and banking establishments occupying streetside frontage, while the center of the building features the core and receptionist area. Above the dominating base, the shaft of the office tower reflects the composite columns that run the length of the perimeter shaft sheathed in aluminum panels, culminating in the cornice and pyramidal top.

Mellon Bank Center

Location: Philadelphia, Pennsylvania, USA
Completion: 1991
Height: 792ft (241.4m)
Stories: 54
Area: 1.2 million ft²
Structure: Mixed
Cladding: Aluminium, glass
Use: Office

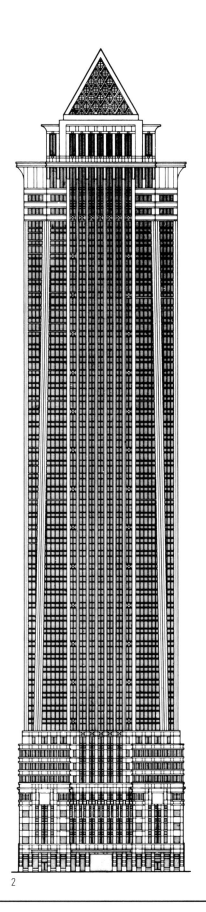

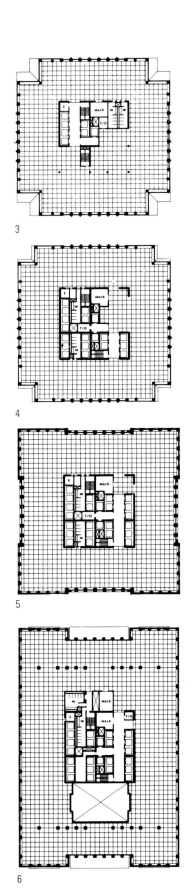

2

6

1 View of Mellon Bank Center (Opposite)
2 North/south elevation
3 Typical high-rise floor plan
4 Typical low-rise floor plan
5 Floors 6–8 typical floor plan
6 Floors 2-3 typical floor plan
Photography: Peter Olson courtesy Kohn Pedersen Fox
Associates

Architect: Kohn Pederson Fox Associates
Structural Engineer: The Office of Irwin G. Cantor
Services Engineer: Flack & Kurtz
Developers: Richard I. Rubin & Company Inc.,
    Equitable Life Insurance, Mellon Bank
Construction Manager: Turner Construction Co.
    New York

Frank Woolworth, farm boy risen to retail tycoon, had a great dream: to build the tallest building in the world bearing his name. On his many visits to London, he was impressed by the Houses of Parliament. He asked Cass Gilbert, an American architect who had studied in Europe, to design an office building in a similar gothic style: spires, gargoyles, flying buttresses, stone traceries. Thus on completion, the building was also called the 'Cathedral of Commerce' and the 'Queen of Manhattan.'

An outstanding masterpiece of the American beaux-arts eclectic period, the Woolworth Building soars 792 feet above Broadway containing 57 stories plus three basement levels. The building has a U-shaped base, 29 stories high, above which the square tower rises with several setbacks. The top is a crown with pinnacles and gargoyles, one of which represents Cass Gilbert holding a model of his building.

The total cost for this Neo-Gothic monument, completed in 1913, was $13.5 million. It was all paid in cash, since Mr. Woolworth wished not to take a mortgage, thereby practicing the same principle as his customers who paid in nickels and dimes. To this day it is almost always fully rented and has never changed hands. Until 1930, when the Chrysler Building was completed, the Woolworth Building was the tallest building in the world.

The structure is covered in polychromed terra-cotta blocks, considered one of the most durable building materials due to its impervious vitreous glazing. The interior as well as the exterior of the building carries the Gothic theme throughout, including polished terrazzo floors, Italian marble, wainscoting, and gilded ornamental work.

Pneumatic caissons were selected for the foundation with an average depth of 110 feet to bedrock. The steel beams and girders were so heavy that surveyors had to test the streets to make sure that no cave-ins would occur during deliveries to the site. The tower was also braced with portal braces for up to 200 mph wind-speed.

The Woolworth Building was the first to have its own power plant, which generates enough electricity for 5,000 people. The high-speed elevator system, comprising 30 cabs, was also the best in the world at the time and could rise 700 feet in a single minute.

F.W. Woolworth Company's offices occupy several floors of the building along with other major clients. In addition, it incorporates a health club, swimming pool, medical and dental facilities, restaurants, and retail stores. In 1981 a major restoration was completed, replacing 26,000 deteriorated terracotta elements with cast stone and cement, matching the originals in color and detail.

Woolworth Building

Location: New York, New York, USA
Completion: 1913
Height: 792ft (241.4m)
Stories: 57
Area: 1.3 million ft²
Structure: Steel
Cladding: Polychromed terracotta blocks
Use: Office

2

3

4

5

6

7

1 Early photo of Woolworth Building (Opposite)
2 View from ground level
3 Terracotta gargoyle
4 Gargoyle of Cass Gilbert holding a model of his building
5 Restoration work begins
6&7 Intricate detailing in foyer
Photography: courtesy Wiss Janney Elstner Associates (1,5); Douglas Mason (2,3,4,6,7)

Architect: Cass Gilbert
Structural Engineer: Gunvald Aus
Developer: Frank W. Woolworth
Owner: Frank W. Woolworth Company
Restoration: The Ehrenkrantz Group & Eckstut
Restoration Contractor: Turner Construction Co.

In 1986 Tokyo's city government decided it was time for a new building to meet its needs. A design competition was held for the new headquarters of Tokyo's metropolitan political government plaza. The design was chosen, along with the architect, structural engineer, services engineer, and all the other professionals involved in the construction of a tall building. The new City Hall was eventually completed in 1991. Today it is not only the dominating skyscraper in Tokyo but one that also acts as a community focus able to accommodate 6,000 people.

The entire complex encompasses three city blocks and is composed of several geometric forms. Two square towers form the skyscraper element rising 797 feet and 48 stories. Between the two towers lies a 34-story tower, which constitutes the administrative area.

These buildings are joined by two passageways extending from the third-floor level of the larger towers. At the base of the buildings a semi-circular plaza, with its colonnades, activates the area. The plaza gradually slopes down towards a center stage. The plaza in its traditional role acts as a forum of exchange between people.

The exterior of the building is covered precast concrete panels, measuring 4 x 3.2 meters. Two different colors of granite are set within the concrete and openings are filled with mirror glass. The two high-rise towers are framed to allow for maximum flexibility in the interior space for technology upgrades in the future.

During the conceptual stage it was suggested that the design looked like a microchip or an electronic circuit. From this point on, the expressionism of the design was geared towards the integration of circuits. The image of the microchip is to be found in the interior on the ceiling, the second floor, and in other parts of the whole.

Since the functions of Tokyo as a city have become increasingly complex and sophisticated, the administration of the metropolitan government is required to focus on efficiency. The complex was successfully completed by allowing for easily manipulated office space. The outward appearance of the complex symbolizes Japan's growing technology, and Tokyo City Hall adds grace to Japan's ever-higher skyline.

Tokyo City Hall

Location: Tokyo, Japan
Completion: 1991
Height: 797ft (242.9m)
Stories: 48
Area: 2 million ft²
Structure: Mixed
Cladding: Precast concrete, granite, mirror glass
Use: Office

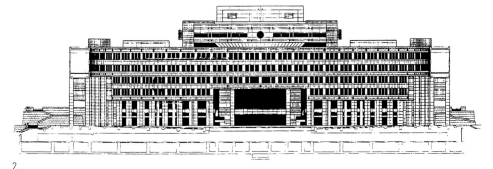

1 View of the towers (Opposite)
2 West elevation
3 Sweeping plaza with colonnades
Photography: Osamu Murai courtesy Kenzo Tange
& Associates

2

3

Architect: Kenzo Tange & Associates
Structural Engineer: Mutoh Associates
Services Engineer: Kenchiku Setsubi Co.
Developer: City of Tokyo
General Contractor: Taisei Kensetsu

This concrete tower was the result of an architectural design competition held in 1979, won by a local architect whose design adapted ideas from traditional Malay architecture into the contemporary form of the tower. Elements of the design suggested associations of form, color, and decorations without being literal. Soon after the project was awarded, the building program changed; the square footage doubled and a rooftop helicopter pad was added. At the same time, the architect was instructed to hold true to the original design.

Although the design of the tower itself was well received, its location near low-rise buildings was not. The eight-acre site allows the building to stand alone from its neighbors, and so its form, with a variety of elements, was designed to visually diminish the scale of the tower. The tower is two overlapping squares in plan, with the overlapping space defining the core of the building, while creating two distinct rental areas on each floor.

The most striking elements of the building are the elevations. They create variety through the use of repetitive elements arranged in varying forms. The solid planes and vertical stripes of windows and structure combine with the tapering elements to form eight elevations which change as one moves around the building. To decrease the apparent volume, the architect utilized the vertical mullions as slimming elements while the slope of the first 12 stories acts as a transition from the smaller scaled neighborhood to the tower. The zig-zag motif of the transfer girders is a structural solution which breaks the monotony of the facade and becomes a decorative element.

The taper is repeated at the top to balance the form. The original design had a pointed silhouette, whereas the built form required the helipad. On the windowless elevations, fire escapes are hung and covered in black to further slim the tower, while emphasizing the joint between the two squares on the elevation. The most traditional feature of the building is the main entrance which features the multi-layered, tapering roof, a symbol of wealth. The construction of the bank was in concrete because local contractors were more experienced in reinforced concrete construction than in steel.

Malayan Bank

Location: Kuala Lumpur, Malaysia
Completion: 1988
Height: 799ft (243.5m)
Stories: 50
Area: 1.8 million ft²
Structure: Concrete
Cladding: Concrete
Use: Office

2

3

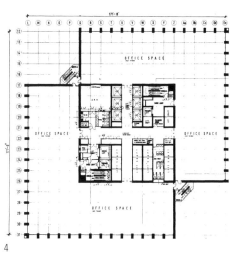

4

1 View of Malayan Bank (Opposite)
2 Spacious banking floor
3 Windowed banking lobby
4 Typical floor plan
Photography: courtesy Hijjas Kasturi Associates Sdn (1,2,3)

Architect: Hijjas Kasturi Associates Sdn
Structural Engineer: Jurutera Konsultant
Services Engineer: Kenchiku Setsubi Co.
Developer: Malayan Banking Berhad
General Contractor: Taisei Kensetsu

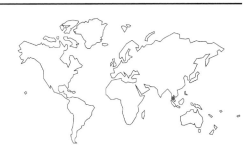

Built in 1963, the 59-story MetLife Building, known for years as the Pan Am Building, was the largest commercial office building of its time, accommodating 250,000 daily visitors and 17,000 office workers.

Located in the heart of Manhattan's East Side along the axis of Park Avenue and connected to Grand Central Terminal, its primary requirement was that it interact well with the urban fabric and facilitate local pedestrian and vehicular circulation.

The building's design team created a circulation network for public spaces, which included a 76-foot-wide thoroughfare with 18 escalators. These escalators provide pedestrian access through the building, linking Park Avenue to Grand Central's rail and subway lines. The mezzanine, which can also be reached by escalator, is lined with shops and restaurants. Fifty-nine elevators serve the upper floors, thus keeping this 'vertical city' confined within short distances. A 400-car garage, open to the public, can be entered from either side of the building.

The octagonal mass of the building, which rises above Grand Central station, caused considerable controversy at the time of its construction, since its location appears to block the perspective from upper Park Avenue.

The 49-story tower of the structure rests on a 10-story base which aligns with the cornice of Grand Central Terminal. The broad sides of the octagonal tower face north and south primarily to reduce the air conditioning loads, but also for aesthetic reasons. The precast concrete panels of the curtain wall are bold in scale and, through its shadows, help to accentuate the movement of light on its surfaces. For years, the roof served as a heliport, providing midtown executives with the option of riding up to the world's tallest 'landing strip' and flying directly to New York's outlying airports.

Within three months of its opening, the building was 92.5% rented, well on its way to proving its success by attracting prestigious tenants into its 2.4 million square feet of floor space.

Since 1981, the Metropolitan Life Insurance Company has owned the building, but it waited until 1992 to dismantle and replace the aluminum and neon 'Pan Am' sign. By that time, Pan Am was no longer in business.

MetLife Building

(Also known as: 200 Park Avenue; formerly: Pan Am Building)

Location: New York, New York, USA
Completion: 1963
Height: 808ft (246.3m)
Stories: 59
Area: 2.4 million ft²
Structure: Steel
Cladding: Precast concrete
Use: Office

2

4

3

1 MetLife Building (Opposite)
2 MetLife in the New York skyline
3 Street-level public space lets MetLife bustle with activity
4 Brilliant flowers greet shoppers
Photography: Douglas Mason

Architects: Emery Roth & Sons
Structural Engineer: The Office of James Ruderman
Services Engineer: Jaros, Baum & Bolles
Design Consultants: Walter Gropius (The Architects
    Collaborative) and Pietro Belluschi
Developer: Erwin Wolfson
General Contractor: Diesel Construction Company
    Inc.
Owner: Metropolitan Life Insurance Company

This 60-story office building for Chase Manhattan Bank is located on a two-and-one-half acre site in lower Manhattan. A plaza covers the multi-level basement, where banking rooms, a cafeteria, garages, and mechanical equipment are located. The City of New York turned over to the bank the street separating two city blocks in return for a wide sidewalk around the perimeter of the site. Taking advantage of the pre-1961 New York City zoning law, which permitted a tower of unlimited height to occupy 25% of the land, Chase was allowed to cover nearly 30% of the land with a massive building without setbacks. The success of its design, along with two other well-known examples of similar concept (the Lever House and the Seagrams Building), resulted in 1961 in a change in zoning, replacing the setbacks of the earlier skyscrapers with the tower and plaza form exemplified by Chase.

The building demonstrated structurally that a long and narrow form could be framed in its short dimension with three spans, the two center columns defining the elevator and service core while the two perimeter columns allowed uninterrupted interior office areas, which could be easily organized for maximum efficiency. Furthermore, proximity to the window wall, which provides a natural light source as well as the superb views, would give it prime rental value.

One Chase Manhattan Plaza was the first major skyscraper to be built to the south of the Brooklyn Bridge, reversing the trend of business moving to midtown. Its glass and aluminum international style architecture stands in stark contrast to its predominantly masonry-covered neighbors. The vertical columns are clad in aluminum and represent the most prominent feature of this minimalist design.

The 89,466-square-foot plaza provides a generous amount of open land in this crowded business district. The plaza and the office building are situated on a black stone podium. On the south side, the plaza is reached by a broad course of 10 steps.

A sculpture fountain is set in a glass-walled well 16 feet below plaza level, called 'The Water Garden.' It consists of a 60-foot diameter pool and fountain, with patterned paving of granite cubes and seven basalt rocks selected from the bottom of the Uji River in Japan. The pool recalls the traditional Japanese garden with its symbolic islands, seas and mountains in miniature. The fountain can produce various effects ranging from a great spray to a serene bubbling movement.

One Chase Manhattan Plaza

Location: New York, New York, USA
Completion: 1961
Height: 813ft (247.8m)
Stories: 60
Area: 2.3 million ft²
Structure: Steel
Cladding: Aluminum, glass
Use: Office

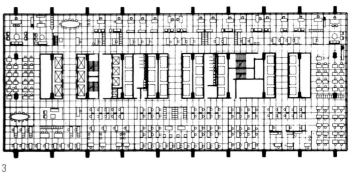

1 Looking up from ground level (Opposite)
2 View of One Chase Manhattan Plaza
3 Typical floor plan
4 Street level
5 One Chase Manhattan Plaza (center) as seen from
   the East River
Photography: courtesy Skidmore, Owings & Merrill (1);
Douglas Mason (2,4); Eric Locker courtesy Skidmore,
Owings & Merrill (5)

Architects: Skidmore, Owings & Merrill (SOM)
Structural Engineer: SOM
Associate Structural Engineer: Weiskopf & Pickworth
Mechanical Engineer: Jaros, Baum & Bolles

Electrical Engineer: Meyer, Strong & Jones
Developer: Chase Manhattan Bank
General Contractor: Turner Construction Company

When it was completed in 1989, CitySpire displaced Metropolitan Tower as the tallest concrete structure in New York City—concrete placement reached to 800 feet (244m) and aluminum-dome fins extended the height to 814 feet (248m) above grade—making it the second tallest concrete structure in the world (it now stands as the 8th tallest concrete building in the world). The building was increased by an additional 26 stories through ingenious creative zoning known as the 'transfer of air rights', developed in the 1970's. According to this regulation, the unused development rights of some Manhattan landmark buildings can be purchased and transferred to new buildings—in this instance, from its neighbor, the City Center, an extravagant, neo-Moorish theater. This mutually beneficial relationship was crucial in rescuing the landmark theater and assuring its financial success. In addition, a three-story wing expansion for the stage was incorporated into the base of CitySpire.

The building rises out of the base in a series of three setbacks, with its octagonal shaft clad in stone, its lateral wings of glass projecting toward the east and west. These wings terminate in an 80-foot-diameter copper dome, responding to the classical tripartite subdivision of the tall building into base, shaft, and top. Below the dome is a large penthouse apartment with 360-degree views.

Envisioned as a return to the romantic image of the earlier skyscrapers, this mixed-use complex contains residential condominiums, retail and commercial offices, and the City Center Theater expansion stage.

Poured-in-place reinforced concrete was used because of its flexibility in a residential area. At the 24th floor, the entire residential structure changes to accommodate the column grid of the office building. With the maximum dimension of its 'structural footprint' of only 80 feet, CitySpire is one of the slenderest skyscrapers in New York.

In March 1991, CitySpire had the "bizarre distinction as the only skyscraper in the world ever cited by New York for whistling", said the *New York Times*. According to reports, the whistle emanating from the building was so loud that people 10 blocks away lost sleep on windy nights. The whistle was later silenced by removing every other louver from the cooling tower. Widening the gap through which the wind 'whistled' effectively silenced the high-pitched noise that some likened to an all-clear signal in London in World War II.

CitySpire

Location: **New York, New York, USA**
Completion: **1989**
Height: **814ft (248.1m)**
Stories: **75**
Area: **830,000 ft²**
Structure: **Concrete**
Cladding: **Concrete, stone, glass**
Use: **Multiple**

2

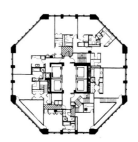

3

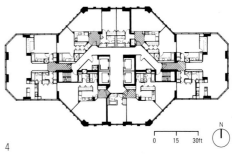

4

5

1 CitySpire shines in the sunlight (Opposite)
2 Bird's-eye view, with Central Park in background
3 Floor plan 69th floor
4 Typical floor plan 47th–60th floor
5 Artist's rendering
Photography: Scott Frances/Esto courtesy Murphy/Jahn Inc.
Architects (1,2)

Architect: Murphy/Jahn Inc. Architects
Structural Engineer: Robert Rosenwasser
  Associates
Services Engineer: Cosentini Associates
Developer: Eichner Properties
Construction Manager: Tishman Construction Corp.
  of New York

With the Melbourne site in development for over thirty years, the completion of the Rialto Towers in 1985 was an engineering and economic success. The design of the two Towers was determined primarily through conformity with regulations regarding such issues as shadow restrictions on the nearby river, a 20-meter setback along the Tower's main Collins Street frontage, and orienting the structure to minimize heat gain on the northern face.

Constructed of reinforced concrete, the two Towers, one 63 stories and the other 43, are linked to become one, even though they function as two. As concrete cures, it experiences shrinkage and creep. In a single building, these effects can be taken into account. But in two Towers of different heights, their overall effect would be different, especially at the top where there was expected a 40mm difference.

The structural engineer's solution was to trick the smaller Tower into believing it was equal in height to its big brother. Through the use of prestressed cables in its columns, the smaller Tower was designed to experience the same vertical loading.

The concrete floor slabs were completed on a six-day cycle. With the load-bearing core and perimeter columns constructed in advance, a floor slab framework was constructed on a floor below and then 'flown' (hoisted) into position. After that, the concrete for the floor slab was poured.

The whole complex is supported by 76 concrete caissons, that reach to bedrock 20 meters below ground. Ninety-five thousand cubic meters of concrete were used to construct Rialto Center.

Melbourne was a city born out of the 1850s gold rush. This wealth brought with it the Victorian style architecture popular in its day. The pedestrian in Melbourne will notice the striking contrast of the Rialto Towers with their Victorian-style neighbors. The Tower, sheathed entirely in blue reflective glass, mirrors the ever changing Australian environment, while proclaiming its modernism.

Rialto Towers

Location: Melbourne, Australia
Completion: 1985
Height: 814ft (248.1m)
Stories: 63
Area: 1.58 million ft²
Structure: Concrete
Cladding: Reflective blue glass
Use: Office

2

3

1 Night falls in Melbourne (Opposite)
2 Rialto Towers stand tall over the Melbourne skyline
3 Rialto Towers reflective blue glass
4 Sunset in the Melbourne skyline
Photography: courtesy David B. Simmonds/Taking Stock
©1997

4

Architect: Gerard de Preu & Partners
Associate Architect: Perrott Lyon Mathieson Pty Ltd
Structural Engineer: W.L. Meinhardt and
  Partner Pty Ltd
Services Engineer: Lincolne Scott Australia
Developers: St. Martins Properties
  and Grollo Australia
General Contractor: Groton Ltd

Sitting on a geographic high point at the edge of the interstate, IBM Tower is visible from every axis in the city, and at night the lighted roof creates a beacon on the Atlanta horizon. Designed as a skyscraper in the Louis Sullivan tradition, it has distinct tripartite subdivisions: base, shaft, and capital. The mass of the building is visually reduced by a textured facade in rose-colored granite, and carefully fenestrated glass, the setbacks and the grouping of floors in bands of three. The architects chose a Post-Modern emphasis with Gothic overtones and tracery predominating.

Above the balconies ornamented with concrete railings and brackets, posts and ornaments of stone act as a cornice for the base. This theme is carried throughout. At the top the transition is heightened by two setbacks that serve as the base for the copper pyramid top and gold cupola.

The shaft, roughly square with a small slice cut off each of its four corners, rises for most of its height without setbacks. The shaft is composed of stone piers of alternating widths and terminates in a series of syncopated setbacks with ornamental finials. The roof has a granite pedestal supporting a copper-clad octagonal pyramid which crowns the Tower and gives it a strong presence over the skyline.

The parking garage is across the street from the Tower, but connected to it by a pedestrian and service access tunnel. The IBM building also features a botanical garden, an amphitheatre, and a plaza with a central fountain. The fountain can be turned off and its platform can be used as a stage, while the grass-covered steps of the amphitheatre serve as seating. A pathway along the eastern edge of a tree-filled garden is lined with a continuous fountain of closely spaced waterjets, further enhancing its setting and connecting to a 'greenway' system that extends through midtown Atlanta.

Built in 1987, the IBM Tower set a new height record for slipforming with its 725-foot concrete core. It is also one of the most complex cores ever designed and built: 2,670 tons of rebar, 6,000 psi concrete (17,550 cubic yards) riddled with penetrations.

IBM Tower

(Also known as: One Atlantic Center)

Location: Atlanta, Georgia, USA
Completion: 1987
Height: 820ft (249.9m)
Stories: 50
Area: 1.1 million ft²
Structure: Mixed
Cladding: Rose-colored granite, glass, copper
Use: Office

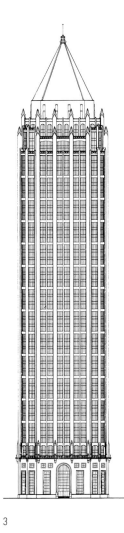

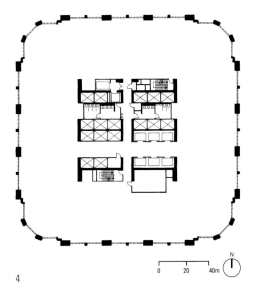

1 Montage of four buildings (IBM photographically inserted)
  (Opposite)
2 IBM Tower
3 Elevation
4 Typical floor plan
5 Artist's rendering of street level
Photography: Courtesy Philip Johnson, Ritchie & Fiore
Architects

0   20   40m

2   3   4

5

Architect: John Burgee Architects and Philip
    Johnson Architects with Heery Architects &
    Engineers, Inc.
Landscape Architect: Zion & Breen Associates Inc.
Structural Engineer: Datum Moore Partnership
Services Engineer: Blum Consulting
Developer: Prentiss Properties
Lead Tenant & Part Owner: IBM
Lighting Consultant: Claude R. Engle

The Osaka World Trade Center (WTC) is a key element in the major Technoport Osaka project, promoted by Osaka City. It is part of an extensive new urban center covering 775 hectares, built on three artificial islands in Osaka Bay known as Maishima, Yumeshima, and Sakishima. The WTC is a major landmark in Cosmo Square. The building has a central role in the city's internationalization and is Osaka's new symbolic landmark.

The building height of 827 feet is the tallest in western Japan. It is clad in a reflective glass curtain wall that emphasizes the white structural elements with its mullions, thus accentuating the verticality of the high-rise tower. At the base it widens out in a triangular shape. The low-rise wing, which includes a 69-foot-high, all-weather atrium, is known as Fespa. Covering an area of 32,290 square feet (3,000 square meters), there is ample room for concerts and festivals. Along with the second floor auditorium, the area is part of a lively public space. This second floor auditorium accommodates 380 people and is used for concerts and exhibitions.

The seventh floor houses conference rooms and business support facilities. Floors 7 through 44 are office floors equipped with the basic functions for a highly computer-oriented building system. Floor-to-ceiling glazed windows offer panoramic views.

The 45th-floor is home of the WTC Museum, featuring photographic exhibitions operated by Japan's International Cooperation Agency. The 48th and 49th floors house the WTC Cosmo Hall, and the Wedding Hall of the 49th offers the highest site designed for marriages in all of Japan. The 48th floor also houses a restaurant, and below, on the 46th and 47th, there are seven additional restaurants featuring international cuisine. The 50th-floor serves as the central facility of the World Trade Center Osaka (WTCO), an international organization offering information to its 400,000 members in major cities around the world.

The top of the building, its 55th-floor, is an observation deck known as the 'Top of the Bay,' offering a 360-degree panoramic view. At night the entire building, spilling light from each of its full-height windows on every floor, shines like a 'pillar of light.'

Osaka World Trade Center

(Formerly: Cosmo Tower)

Location: Osaka, Japan
Completion: 1995
Height: 827ft (252.1m)
Stories: 55
Area: 160,700 ft²
Structure: Steel
Cladding: Reflective glass
Use: Office

2

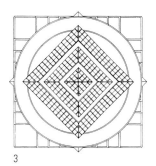

3

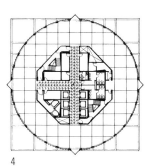

4

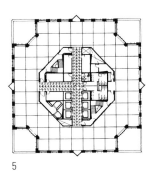

5

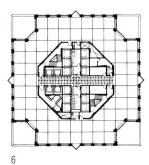

6

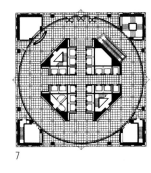

7

1 Geometric theme is carried out at one of the Messeturm entrances (Opposite)
2 Messeturm means 'fair tower'
3 Roof plan
4 High–rise cylinder plan
5 High–rise plan
6 Low–rise plan
7 Ground floor plan
8 Glass panels of lobby
9 Street level
Photography: courtesy Murphy/Jahn Inc. Architects

8

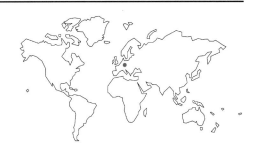

9

Architect: Murphy/Jahn Inc. Architects
Structural Engineers: Dr Ing. Fritz Noetzold,
  The Office of Irwin G. Cantor
Services Engineers: Brendel Ingenieure, Jaros,
  Baum & Bolles
Electrical Engineer: Ebener & Partner
Developer: Tishman Speyer Properties

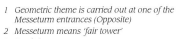

The smaller tower in the two-tower Liberty Place complex, Two Liberty Place complements the aesthetic impact of the first tower and the economic requirements of the developer. Whereas One Liberty Place is basically a square tower, two Liberty Place is essentially rectangular in plan to accommodate the larger square footage's required. This is accomplished with a partial-height bustle which is attached to a square tower similar to the first tower. As Two Liberty Place enters the skyline the bustle stops to reveal a square shaft and gable top, creating a dialogue with the first tower, while maintaining a distinct identity.

The building meets the ground with a three-story stone podium, which houses the lobby for the tower and entrances to the retail complex lining the two towers. Above the base, the shaft is composed of two distinct elements: the square of the original tower, and the bustle. The square portion has polished stone cladding whereas the bustle is sheathed in glass to emphasize its attachment to the original form. The gabled top, while reminiscent to One Liberty Place, is not identical—thereby creating the interaction between the towers. The crown of Two Liberty Place is defined by a single gable with a small spire, whereas One Liberty Place features multiple gables and a tall spire. The structure of the building utilizes outrigger frames to resist lateral forces. The location of the outriggers was determined by the three banks of elevators arranged linearly within the building.

The Liberty Place complex is the first to rise above the 491-foot height limit, the top of the William Penn statue atop City Hall, and dramatically redefined the Philadelphia skyline. After the completion of One Liberty Place, the construction of Two Liberty Place was well received by the community, and was rented by a single firm before construction was completed. Construction of Two Liberty Place coincided with the construction of the retail complex and a four-star hotel.

For futher information regarding Liberty Place Complex, please see page 164.

Two Liberty Place

Location: Philadelphia, Pennsylvania, USA
Completion: 1990
Height: 848ft (258.5m)
Stories: 58
Area: 1.2 million ft²
Structure: Steel
Cladding: Stone, glass
Use: Office

3

4

2

1 Two Liberty Place (Opposite)
2 Axonometric view Of Liberty Place complex
3 Two Liberty Place under construction
4 Liberty Place glows red in the setting sun
Photography: Matt Wargo courtesy Murphy/Jahn Inc.
Architects (1,3,4)

Architect: Murphy/Jahn Inc. Architects
Associate Architect: Zeidler Roberts Partnership
Structural Engineer: Quinn Dressel
Services Engineer: ECE Group
Developer: The Rouse Associates

The 70-story G.E. Building is the centerpiece of the Rockefeller Center complex, built by John D. Rockefeller, Jr, founder of Standard Oil. The Center has been called a 'city within a city,' the nation's most successful urban complex, the most welcome oasis, and the city's unofficial 'village green.' In 1985, the New York City Landmark Preservation Committee bestowed on it landmark status, referring to it as "the heart of New York, a great unifying presence in the chaotic core of midtown Manhattan."

The G.E. Building, with its 850-foot slender silhouette, marked the emergence of a new form of the skyscraper. This thin slab was based on the principle of 27 feet of lighting depth to give optimum working conditions around the central elevator core. Facing north and south, the building presents its huge, broad sides to the street; for this reason, the New York City Guide of 1939 nicknamed the structure "the slab."

This new form of the skyscraper as a 'slab' has been considered by historians to be as significant and as expressive for its period as were the monolith obelisk of Egypt and the Gothic cathedral towers for their respective eras.

The main lobby of the G.E. Building is decorated with an immense mural depicting, in an abstract and allegorical manner, humanity's progress. Installed in 1941, the three large figures represent Past, Present, and Future, who are shown with their feet braced against the large marble columns of the lobby. Other murals in the lobby area include the Spirit of Dance, installed in 1937, and Man's Triumph in Communication–Radio, Telephone and Telegraph–also installed in 1937, on the south side of the first elevator bank.

Rockefeller Center as a whole is the world's largest privately owned business and entertainment center, part of a 22-acre complex in midtown. One of the best examples of Art Deco style, seen in its buildings and their amenities, it features 30 works by this century's great artists. Originally, the Center included 14 buildings and covered 12 acres of land between 48th and 51st Streets. Today there are 19 buildings that occupy almost twice the area.

One of the largest projects ever undertaken by private enterprise at the time of construction, the Center required the demolition of 228 buildings and the relocation of 4,000 tenants. Over 75,000 workers were employed on the building site. Furthermore, for each of those workers actually present on the site, there were two others preparing material elsewhere—which adds up to almost a quarter million employed in the project during the worst years of America's great depression.

G.E. Building

(Formerly: RCA Building; also 30 Rockefeller Center)

Location: New York, New York, USA
Completion: 1933
Height: 850ft (259.1m)
Stories: 70
Area: 2.1 million ft²
Structure: Steel
Cladding: Limestone
Use: Office

3

4

5

7

1 Transamerica Corporate Headquarters catches the final sunset rays (Opposite)
2 Architecturally different, the tower stands out in the skyline (Opposite)
3 Towering above San Francisco
4 Triangular form
5 Public courtyard
6 Detail of facade
7 Public courtyard with fountain
Photography: Mark Snyder (3); Barrie Rokeach (4); Wayne Thom (5)

6

Architect: William L. Pereira Associates
Structural Engineer: Chin and Hensolt
Services Engineer: Simonson & Simonson
Developer: Transamerica Corporation
General Contractor: Dinwiddie Construction Company

The BCE Place complex consists of two office towers, Canada Trust Tower at 856 feet and Bay Wellington Tower at 679 feet. Several historically significant buildings on the site are linked to the Towers by a glass enclosed gallery. Below ground, the complex is connected to Union Station, the underground pedestrian walkway system, and parking garages. The 42-foot-wide and 380-foot-long glazed Galleria was designed by sculptor/architect Santiago Calatrava. The Galleria links the two Towers, a garden court, the below grade retail concourse, and the Hockey Hall of Fame.

Both towers are clad in flamed Rockville pink granite with polished Cambrian black granite accents and green tinted glass. Inside, the two-story retail podium at the base of Canada Trust Tower is richly adorned with marble floors and walls. Typical floors have full-height windows and nine-foot ceilings. The Tower's location on the outskirts of the central commercial district provides panoramic views in all directions, and the overlapping squares of the floor plan allows for numerous corner offices. The Tower's construction in 1990 coincided with a boom in the Toronto market in new commercial real estate in the downtown area.

Canada Trust Tower

Location: Toronto, Canada
Completion: 1990
Height: 856ft (260.9m)
Stories: 53
Area: 1.5 million ft²
Structure: Mixed
Cladding: Granite, glass
Use: Office

2

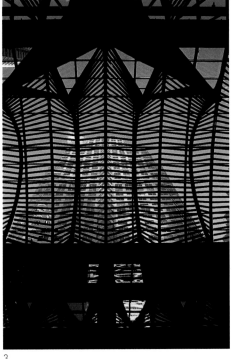

3

4

5

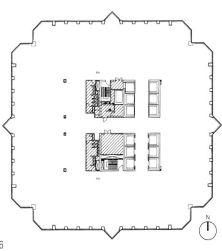

6

1 Canada Trust Tower (left) is part of the BCE Place complex
   including a second lower Tower called Bay Wellington
   Tower (right) (Opposite)
2 A grand entrance for pedestrians
3 View of Tower from Galleria
4 The majestic Galleria links the two Towers
5 Tower entrance
6 Typical floor plan
Photography: Robert Burley/Design Archive courtesy
Bregman + Hamann Architects (1,4); Ivan Zaknic (2,3,5)

Architects: Bregman + Hamann Architects, Skidmore
    Owings & Merrill (in joint venture)
Structural Engineer: M.S. Yolles & Partners
Mechanical Engineer: The Mitchell Partnership
Electrical Engineer: Mulvey & Banani International
Developer: Brookfield Development Corporation
Contractor: PCL Constructors Eastern, Inc.

When the news release was issued in 1972, First Interstate Tower, then known as United California Bank (UCB) Corporate Headquarters Building, was touted to be the tallest building in the United States west of Chicago. When complete it would punctuate the downtown skyline of Los Angeles at 858 feet (262m).

The location for the Tower in the northwest corner of Wilshire Boulevard at Hope Street is the former site of one of Los Angeles' first commercial skyscrapers. The building served as the headquarters for the Western Bancorporation, which at the time had 23 affiliated banks, serving 355 communities in 11 western states.

First Interstate Tower sits on a spacious landscaped plaza paved in gray granite. It tapers inward 5.5 feet from the street level to the top. At its base, massive L-shaped aluminum-clad piers 12 feet wide anchor the building at its four corners. Above it, projecting bronze aluminum mullions and bronze solar glass windows and spandrels rise the full height of the structure, dramatizing the verticality of its design. The steel-frame structure features one of the largest steel columns ever used in Los Angeles, measuring three feet at the lower levels and weighing more than one ton per foot. The foundation for the tower is a structural steel frame on mat and bell cassions.

At the ground level an uninterrupted space serves as the banking floor. The building's 27 high-speed elevators start from the mezzanine lobby area above the banking level. Two private elevators connect the main banking levels to the seventh floor.

An underground pedestrian concourse and vehicular tunnel connect the three below-grade levels. Three floors of underground parking accommodate 340 cars, and a 10-story-high structure provides an additional 760 car parking spaces, and a first-floor commercial space.

On May 4, 1988, while the sprinkler system was being installed, a fire which started on the 12th-floor destroyed five floors, killing one person and injuring 40. It took 300 fire fighters almost four hours to control the blaze. Since that time, all of Los Angeles' tall buildings are required to be fitted with sprinkler systems.

First Interstate Tower

(Formerly: United California Bank)

Location: Los Angeles, California, USA
Completion: 1974
Height: 858ft (261.5m)
Stories: 62
Area: 1.25 million ft²
Structure: Steel
Cladding: Aluminium, glass
Use: Office

1 First Interstate Tower knifes the sky (Opposite)
2 View of First Interstate Tower
3 The tower stands tall in Los Angeles
4 View from ground level
Photography: courtesy The Luckman Partnership (1,2);
Ivan Zacnic (2,3)

3

2

4

Architect: The Luckman Partnership
Structural Engineer: Erkel Greenfield Associates Inc.
Services Engineer: Levine & McCann
Electrical Engineer: Michael Garris & Associates

Developers: United California Bank Realty
Corporation and The Equitable Life Insurance
Society of the U.S.
General Contractor: C.L. Peck

Water Tower Place bears the name of its illustrious neighbor, the historic Chicago Water Tower and Pumping Station built in 1869 in imitation Gothic. The Water Tower Station—which Oscar Wilde called a "castellated monstrosity"—actually survived the Great Fire of 1871 and remains a part of Chicago's history today.

Water Tower Place was the world's tallest concrete building at the time of its completion in 1976, built at a cost of $150 million. It retained that title until 1990.

The Tower rises from the back of a seven-story retail shopping mall with its 74 stories wrapped round a central atrium. It also houses the Ritz-Carlton Hotel, 40 condominiums, office space, parking for 640 cars, the Carlton Club, several restaurants, and seven movie theaters.

In many respects, this building appears to be one of the most complicated in Chicago, with its diverse accommodations and its unprecedented offering: a whole city within a city block. Its bulk and diversity—a result of laissez-faire attitude toward zoning—meant that it became the catalyst for the phenomenal growth in economic prosperity and urban vitality in this micro-area of Chicago. It is reported that Water Tower Place draws over 12 million visitors annually, who spend some $800,000 per day.

Three separate but complementary building transportation systems, with a combined capacity of more than 18,000 persons per hour, carry shoppers through the seven floors of this vertical city.

The massing of the building's lower floors resulted from the retailers' demand that there be no windows in the seven-story retail space. However, generous amounts of light are brought into its interior through the Grand Atrium and two light courts on the east and west. Glass-enclosed elevators carry shoppers to all seven floors.

Water Tower Place was the first new mixed-use development in the area. It used up to 9,000 psi concrete in columns. In 1976, it was at the cutting edge of high-strength concrete. By using concrete instead of steel, the building could be 90 feet shorter for the same number of floors—thus saving the substantial cost associated with the enclosing of the exterior envelope in marble and glass. Because of their pioneering use of high-strength concrete, the architects received a major grant from the National Science Foundation to place monitors in the structural steel frame of the building to measure long-term shortening.

Water Tower Place

Location: Chicago, Illinois, USA
Completion: 1976
Height: 859ft (261.8m)
Stories: 74
Area: 3.1 million ft²
Structure: Concrete
Cladding: Concrete
Use: Multiple

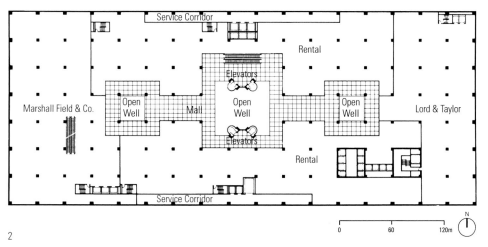

Service Corridor

Rental

Elevators

Marshall Field & Co.

Open Well

Mall

Open Well

Open Well

Lord & Taylor

Elevators

Rental

Service Corridor

0   60   120m

N

1   Until 1990, Water Tower Place was the tallest reinforced concrete building in the world (Opposite)
2   Commercial 3rd, 5th, and 7th floors
3   Atrium-covered shopping area
4   A prototype for mixed-use development
Photography: David Clifton courtesy Loebl Schlossman & Hackl/Hague Richards (1,4); Ivan Zaknic (3)

2

3

4

Architect: Loebl Schlossman, Bennett, & Dart
Consultant Architect: Warren Platner Associates
    (commercial space)
Structural Engineer: C.F. Murphy Associates
Services Engineer: C.F. Murphy Associates
    (Lou Moro, Project Engineer)

Developer: JMB/Urban Investment & Development
    Company
General Contractor: Inland Robbins Construction, Inc.
Concrete Supplier: James McHugh Construction Co.

Retail, hotel, office, residence—all in one place! It sounds like a whole city, but this mixed-use 67-story building contains them all in one structure, enclosing 2.7 million square feet in this busy shopping area on Chicago's north side.

The designers honored the tradition of Chicago architecture by placing low volume directly along North Michigan Avenue, and by applying the classical tripartite composition to articulate the mass of the building.

The base is a street-defining element containing retail, office and part of the hotel space, the middle or tower portion with its vertical thrust encloses the hotel and residential parts, and the top terminates with four corner pavilions and lanterns. The designers combined modern structural and classical compositional techniques with Art Deco elegance of the 1930s. A four-story atrium is clad in limestone granite and marble to add visual interest at street level. The design of the base uses cornice lines to emphasize the human scale and to integrate the storefronts with the facade of the building.

The office tenants have their own separate lobby on Walton Street. From the ground floor they take a high-speed elevator to the sky lobby and then to their offices. The 48th through 66th floors contain the tower residences, 125 condominiums served by elevators from a private lobby. The retail portion includes a 220,000-square-foot Bloomingdale's, the first in the midwest. Behind the retail portion there is a parking garage.

In addition to the above amenities, there are also private dining facilities, meeting and boardrooms, and a health spa as well as restaurants, movie theaters, and a grand ballroom—all accessible without leaving the building.

This truly mixed-use building also employs mixed construction. Two framing systems (moment-frame tube and moment-resistant tube) and the two basic materials (steel and concrete) created a highly successful economic hybrid structure. Crowning the building are pyramidal turrets made of steel tube frames and clad with copper sheathing.

At the top of the tower the residential floors are flat concrete slabs with structural columns 15 to 20 feet apart. Between the 47th and 48th floors, concrete wall girders transfer these columns to a larger span of 30 feet, and at the 30th floor, the upper concrete structure transfers to steel below it. Finally at the seventh floor, the grid shifts again to a braced frame which continues down to the foundations.

900 North Michigan Avenue

Location: Chicago, Illinois, USA
Completion: 1989
Height: 871ft (265.5m)
Stories: 66
Area: 2.7 million ft²
Structure: Mixed
Cladding: Granite, marble
Use: Multiple

2

3

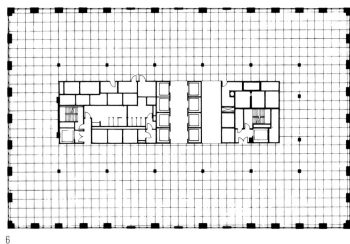

5

6

1 View of building (Opposite)
2 Pyramidal turrets at top of 900 North Michigan Avenue
3 Main entrance
4 Interior atrium
5 Model
6 Floor plan
Photography: Hedrich-Blessing courtesy
Kohn Pedersen Fox Associates (1,3); Ivan Zaknic (2); Wayne Cable
courtesy Kohn Pedersen Fox Associates (4)

**Architects: Perkins & Will Architects, with Kohn
    Pedersen Fox Associates**
Structural Engineer: Alfred Benesch & Company
Services Engineer: Environmental System Design Inc.
**Developer: J.M.B. Urban Investment and
    Development Co.**
**General Contractor: J.A. Jones Construction
    Company, C.M. Inland**

**Construction Company: Walsh Construction Co.
    of Illinois (parking)**

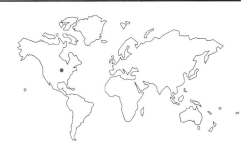

In the geographic, historic, and economic center of Charlotte, the tallest tower in the southeastern United States rises as the focal point of the skyline. While the developers saw the tower as a symbol of profit, the architect envisioned the tower as much more.

The developers' program for the property called for a maximum of height, efficiency, and economy in the building. This was achieved using poured-in-place concrete construction which achieved 12 foot-8 inch floor-to-floor heights and 48-foot column free spans between the core and the perimeter.

The architect used this opportunity to create a unique presence which would revitalize the downtown area. Symbolized by the filigreed cagework atop the tower, dubbed the crown of the 'Queen City,' the tower provides the economic cornerstone for a large, public complex. The complex consists of the tower, two landscaped plazas and 'Founder's Hall,' a glass-enclosed mall with retail shops lining its perimeter. It is connected to the Blumenthal Performing Arts Center and the Overstreet Mall, as well as a parking garage across the street accessed by way of a pedestrian bridge.

The base is sheathed in dark granite with marble columns at the entrances. The extensive use of stone throughout the lower floors symbolizes stability. The shaft features vertically organized slots of windows interspersed with piers of warm, beige granite which become progressively narrower and thinner at each setback. The main elevations are slightly curved and step back as the tower rises. The top culminates in a filigreed cagework composed of silver vertical rods. During the day this cagework reflects the sunlight, whereas it is lit from within at night. As the architect described it: "Charlotte is a city being remade, almost anew. There are very, very few old buildings. So one is dealing with a rather clean slate. The task was not one of relating to a specific context, but only to do a very beautiful tower expressing the self perceptions of NCNB."

Reinforced concrete was selected because of its ability to support the loads while allowing the smaller floor-to-floor height. The system used was also less expensive than a combination steel and concrete system. Although the system exceeded North Carolina wind loads requirements, because of national seismic requirements steel was added to the columns and beams along with diagonal bracing at the setbacks. Heavier loads on the core columns required the initial floor construction to be sloped while the columns cured.

NationsBank Corporate Center

(Formerly: NCNB Tower)

Location: Charlotte, North Carolina, USA
Completion: 1992
Height: 871ft (265.5m)
Stories: 60
Area: 1.4 million ft²
Structure: Concrete
Cladding: Granite
Use: Office

2

3

4

5

6

7

1 NationsBank Corporate Center at night (Opposite)
2 Looking up to building from south
3 Looking from northwest facade at roof details
4 Looking east in main foyer; art center through window
5 Lift lobby
6 Landscaped plaza at dusk
7 Founders Hall at 'overstreet' level, box office and entrances
  to smaller theaters on left hand side
Photography: Tim Griffith courtesy The Images Publishing
Group Pty Ltd

Architect: Cesar Pelli & Associates
Associate Architect: HKS Inc.
Structural Engineer: Walter P. Moore & Associates
Services Engineer: BL&P Engineers, Inc.
Developers: Lincoln Property Company,
    NationsBank Corporation, and Charter Properties
General Contractor: McDevitt & Street

The Peachtree Center district in Atlanta began as a vision and has grown to become a very prosperous 'city-within-a-city.' The district's success can be attributed to its favorable mix of a dynamic business center with a pedestrian-focused environment of open atriums, plazas, fountains and sculpture gardens. Peachtree Center is more than a commercial or retail district; it is a retreat from many of the typical urban scenes. At the gateway of this new district is SunTrust Plaza at One Peachtree Center. This building is well-situated relative to Atlanta's strong attractions. It is within walking distance of the city's most influential organizations and sporting complexes as well as the financial district and state and local government.

This 871-foot, 60-story point tower is a unique combination of contemporary and classical styles, designed to reflect the architectural characteristics of the entire Peachtree complex. The intricately articulated stepped tower with its strong vertical lines and alternating bays echoes the style of its neighboring buildings. The building uses rich materials, such as two shades of gray glass, to achieve a design representative of Atlanta's modern theme.

The interior of SunTrust Plaza displays the same sense of quality and identity as does the exterior facade. To answer the currently rising corporate standards, each floor can successfully adapt and accommodate all types of firms. Floors range from 21,500–27,000 square feet with a central core and curtainwall design to minimize structural interference of the interior and to maximize spatial configurations and options. As is shown by the successive bays on the exterior facades, the tower can have up to 36 corner offices on an average floor, with unmatched views and highly personalized interiors.

Located at the ground level and on each side of the tower, four large granite pavilions mark the entrances as well as a visual link to its highly landscaped grounds. SunTrust Plaza's grand pedestrian space is defined and easily identified by its strong geometric influences. The square footprint of the building is centered in a simple circular reflecting pool. The pool, in turn, acts as a transition to the triangular boundaries of the two-acre site. Tree-lined walkways encircle the area with well-placed fountains and grass courts providing ample space for leisure. The plaza is linked with a uniquely designed fan-shaped staircase, to Peachtree Center Avenue and its series of cafes, shops and restaurants. The staircase also acts as a backdrop for cultural events open to the public.

SunTrust Plaza

(Formerly: One Peachtree Center)

Location: Atlanta, Georgia, USA
Completion: 1992
Height: 871ft (265.5m)
Stories: 60
Area: 1.4 million ft²
Structure: Concrete
Cladding: Gray glass
Use: Office

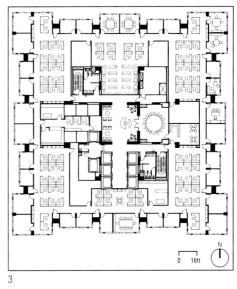

Shuttle Elevator

High Rise Elevator

High-Mid Rise Elevators

Low-Mid Rise Elevators

Low Rise Elevators

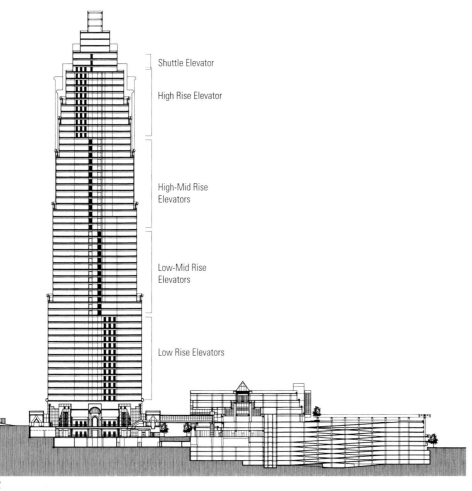

2

1   SunTrust Plaza (Opposite)
2   Elevation of tower
3   Office tower tenant layout
4&5   Dramatic lighting
6   Artwork enhances the beautiful atmosphere
Photography: Michael Portman courtesy John Portman
& Associates (1,4,5); Tim Hursley courtesy John
Portman & Associates (6)

3

4

5

6

Architect/Engineer: John Portman & Associates
Landscape Architect: Arnold Associates
Structural Engineer: John Portman & Associates
Services Engineer: Newcomb & Boyd
Developer: Portman Properties
Owner: Peachtree 400 Assoc. Ltd
Contractor: J.A. Jones

This shimmering glass tower, built in 1975 as the First International Building, experienced a 'rebirth' of sorts 12 years later with the addition of a 172-foot roof-top structure, the renovation of its glass facade, and a name change to Renaissance Tower.

The 1.9 million-square-foot tower was designed with a trussed tube structural system utilizing large 'X' braces each covering 28 floors, two per side of the four-sided building. The renovation of the glass cladding expressed those X braces with blue and green double X's superimposed on a silver background. Lighting at night delineates the exterior cross-bracing, creating two 28-story X's on each side of the tower.

Originally a flat-topped skyscraper in the International Style tradition popular in the 1970s, a 160-foot central spire and four smaller spires were added to the roof in 1987. The steel structure of the spires, painted white, is illuminated at night with vertical shafts of lighting reflecting from glass prisms at the tops of the five spires.

The tower is part of a large financial complex in downtown Dallas. Located on 2.5 acres, the total complex includes the Renaissance Tower, Interfirst Tower, and an 11-story parking garage. Originally at the base of the building there was a drive-up banking facility, which was replaced during the renovations with a nine-story glass pyramid atrium. Beneath the glass atrium is an underground retail and restaurant court which connects to a city-wide underground retail mall.

The trussed tube design of Renaissance Tower was the first time such a system had been used in the southwestern United States. Its advantages were that it eliminated the need for interior bracing and was more economical than conventional framing. The further use of innovative stub-girder design in the tower provided openings in the floor girders for mechanical ducts and eliminated expensive reinforced web openings, resulting in reduced framing weight and floor height, and thus resulting in a savings on material costs. The building was topped out 66 weeks from groundbreaking and 10 months from the erection of the first piece of structural steel.

Renaissance Tower features tandem elevators for building transportation. The 24-passenger elevator shafts each have two elevator cabs, mounted one atop another, moving on a single set of cables. The 1987 renovation included the installation of life-safety, energy management, security, and shared telecommunications services, as well as installation of a marble base and new entrance portals.

Renaissance Tower

(Formerly: First International Building)

Location: Dallas, Texas, USA
Completion: 1975
Height: 886ft (270.1m)
Stories: 56
Area: 1.9 million ft²
Structure: Steel
Cladding: Reflective glass
Use: Office

2

3

4

5

6

1   Front entrance to Renaissance Tower (Opposite)
2   Renaissance Tower, featuring spires and X-bracing
3   View of the retail atrium
4   Interior of atrium
5   Retail atrium and plaza
6   Elevators
Photography: Joe C. Aker courtesy Skidmore Owings & Merrill
(1,3,4,5); Esto courtesy Skidmore, Owings & Merrill (2,6)

Architects: Hellmuth, Obata & Kassabaum; Harwood K. Smith and Partners; Skidmore, Owings & Merrill (1987 renovation)
Structural Engineer: Ellisor and Tanner, Inc.
Services Engineer: Blum Consultants
Construction Manager: Henry C. Beck

Developers: First National Bank, Dallas Management Services, and Prudential Insurance Company of America (joint venture)

A soaring structure 901 feet high, some 500 feet taller than its neighbors, Transco Tower rises alone from a grassy podium, covered with mirrored and non-reflective glass.

The Tower looks back to a golden era of skyscrapers. It recreates the Art Deco style of the 1930s, with the distinct tripartite shape put forth by Louis Sullivan (1896). The inspiration was the Panhellenic Hotel of 1928 in New York City, by John Mead Howells. Both clients, Gerald Hines and Transco Energy Company, wanted a landmark building, and both wanted a structure that reminded them of the Empire State Building. What they got was unique; a perfectly symmetrical tower, with no front or back, "because it stood alone, visible from all angles," said Robert Reinhold, *New York Times*, 1983.

At the lower floors of the base the architects created a huge ceremonial arched doorway 75 feet high, covered in Spanish pink granite. By means of this super-archway, the architects reinforced Houston's favorite promenade, greeting 3,200 cars into the 12-story garage provided on site. The five-story base of the building provides space for a bank on the ground floor as well as extra room on the levels above. It also includes a health club, company cafeteria, and Transco's computer spaces. Inside, the lobby floors are lined with granite and each elevator car is lined with a different colored marble.

The shaft or main body of the Tower is arranged in a progressive series of setbacks, in the tradition of the Art Deco style. Sheathed in two types of glass, the high-tech skin of the shaft mirror and gray tint conveys an ambiguity: is this a stone or a glass tower? The mirrored panels play the role of traditional stone, given their opaque quality, and depending on the time of day might appear blue, green, gray, or black. This is a stone-like building in glass. At sunset, the building resembles a shimmering 'gold ingot', as observed by the vice-president of Transco, William H. Cook.

The top of the building culminates in a low, flattened pyramidal cap, sitting on a square base which contains communications' satellite dishes. The architects made heroic efforts to hide these dishes, rather than allow them to disfigure the elegant design of this contemporary high-tech landmark. The overall effect of the building is a "steeple of a suburban village," as described by John Burgee.

Within the park, covering three acres, there is a jogging trail and, facing the Tower some 300 feet away, a horseshoe-shaped waterfall and fountain 64 feet high, with a roman-arched pediment acting as a foil in front of it. On both sides of the green lawn are planted rows and rows of oak trees, visually connecting the beautiful grounds with the shimmering Transco Tower.

Transco Tower

Location: Houston, Texas, USA
Completion: 1983
Height: 901ft (274.6m)
Stories: 64
Area: 1.6 million ft²
Structure: Steel
Cladding: Mirrored glass
Use: Office

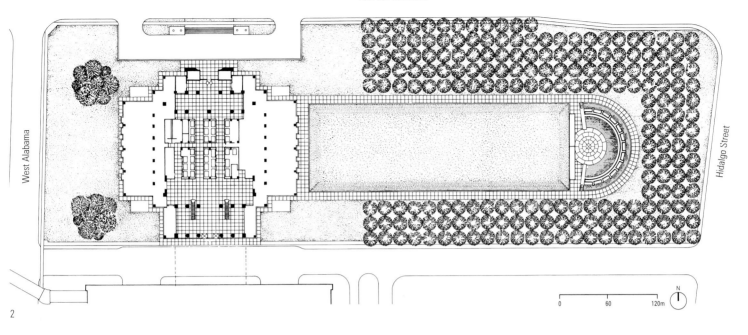

Post Oak Boulevard

West Alabama

Hidalgo Street

2

0   60   120m

N

3

4

1 Building at sunset (Opposite)
2 Site plan
3 Transco Tower and gardens
4 Roman arch entrance way to waterfall at night
Photography: Richard Payne (1,3); Richard Payne
courtesy Johnson/Burgee Architects (4)

Architect: John Burgee Architects with Philip Johnson Architects
Associate Architect: Morris/Aubry
Landscape Architect: Zion & Breen
Structural Engineer: CBM Engineers
Services Engineer: I.A. Naman & Associates
General Contractor: J.A. Jones Construction Company
Project Manager: J.A. Jones Construction Company

Sheathed entirely in red granite and dark glass, Scotia Plaza's distinctive sawtooth design stands in stark contrast to its modern neighbors. Built for the Bank of Nova Scotia, which owns the entire block, the tower includes links to the Bank's original headquarters. During construction the facades of other historic buildings on the site were dismantled and reconstructed for other street frontages.

A glass enclosure projects out from the base of the tower and features commercial and retail spaces as well as links to the other buildings. The canopy of this enclosure extends to the street frontages to redefine the tower's street presence, and to protect pedestrians from down drafts from the tower. The exterior is a polished red granite which is also used throughout the interior. Inside, the main banking hall is lit from above by an 11-story atrium. Below grade is a public concourse, a service floor, and four levels of parking. Typical office floors feature floor-to-ceiling windows. HVAC systems in the ceiling allow occupants to place furniture directly against the exterior walls. The system is individually operated, allowing tenants complete control of their own spaces. Twenty-two double-decker elevators ensure one of the shortest waits of any major skyscraper.

The structure of the building utilizes an exterior wall tube structure which absorbs most of the loading, while allowing for a smaller concrete core as necessitated by the slim floor plan. These elements are linked by a steel floor system. During construction, an off-site pump sent enriched concrete under major streets to the top of the tower where it was poured into frameworks. Eleven hours after pouring, the forms were removed and raised independent of cranes. This freed the cranes to hoist steel, deck, and other building materials, allowing the contractor to complete a floor every two and a half days.

Scotia Plaza

Location: Toronto, Canada
Completion: 1989
Height: 902ft (274.9m)
Stories: 68
Area: 1.6 million ft²
Structure: Mixed
Cladding: Granite, glass
Use: Office

2

1 Scotia Plaza (Opposite)
2 Sawtooth design begins to emerge
3 Foyer lighting
4 Reception desk
Photography: Tony Whibley/UFx Productions courtesy
The Webb Zerafa Menkes Housden Partnership (1);
courtesy Campeau Corporation (2); Ivan Zacnic (3,4)

3

4

Architect: The Webb Zerafa Menkes Housden
Partnership
Structural Engineer: Quinn, Dressel, & Associates
Services Engineer: The Mitchell Partnership
Developer: Campeau Corporation
General Contractor: PCL Construction

From the very beginning, Citicorp Center was an engineering challenge. The block chosen for the site was fully purchased except for one corner: St. Peter's Lutheran Church. The church agreed to sell Citicorp its air rights, on the provision that a new church be designed and constructed on that corner, with no connection to Citicorp and no columns to pass through the church.

The resulting design was a masterpiece. In order to provide light at street level, the columns which support the office tower were shifted to the centers of the facades. The four columns and a center core are what hold up the tower, which is cantilevered 72 feet off each side of the four columns. These columns rise to a height of 114 feet, where the first floor of the tower begins. Located partially under the tower is a seven-story low-rise portion, which steps back as it rises.

The 55-story office tower is a square-shaped sheath covered in alternating bands of aluminum spandrels and silver-tinted reflective glass. The aluminum-clad crown of the building faces south and is sloped on a 45-degree angle.

The church forms a rock-like sculpture, and is covered in red-brown granite. This 'lantern' has a sloped roof that is bisected diagonally by a clear strip of glass skylight that continues down the sides to the base.

The steel frame of Citicorp Center has diagonal wind bracing on the perimeter, which is repeated in eight-story modules. On the floor below, where the diagonal bracing intersect the corners, there are no vertical columns. This is to avoid accumulating gravity load in the corner columns and allows for the bonus feature of unobstructed views.

This building was one of the first tall buildings in the United States to contain a tuned-mass-damper (TMD). This 400-ton computer controlled concrete inertia block controls wind sway movement.

As masterful in design and form as Citicorp is, its story could not be fully told without relating the events of the summer of 1978. Through a series of circumstances, the building's structural engineer discovered a previously undetected flaw that led him to believe the tower would not be able to withstand strong quartering winds. It appeared that the bolted joints, weakest on the building's 30th floor, might tear apart in a severe storm—one that statistics predicted might occur once every 16 years. After three months of frenzied calculations, discussions, and overtime by a cadre of welders, steel reinforcing plates were placed over the bolted joints—permanently correcting the problem and allowing Citicorp Center to preserve its place as a glittering addition to the New York skyline.

Citicorp Center

Location: New York, New York, USA
Completion: 1977
Height: 915ft (278.9m)
Stories: 59
Area: 1.3 million ft²
Structure: Steel
Cladding: Aluminum, reflective glass
Use: Multiple

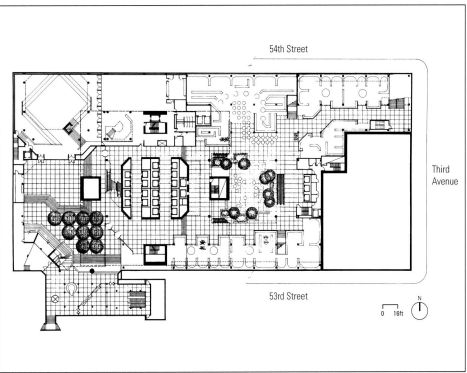

3

4

54th Street

Third
Avenue

53rd Street

N

0   16ft

5

6

1   Looking up (Opposite)
2   Plaza (Opposite)
3   Plaza
4   Concourse plan
5   View of Citicorp Center
6   Street activity
Photography: Norman McGrath courtesy The Stubbins
Associates (1,2); Douglas Mason (3,5,6)

Architect: Hugh Stubbins and Associates/Emory Roth
Structural Engineers: William LeMessurier and
**   Associates/Office of James Ruderman**
Services Engineer: Joseph R. Loring & Associates
Developer: Citibank
General Contractor: HRH Construction

This skyscraper was designed for Raffles Place, Singapore, as the home of the Overseas Union Bank and as a prestigious center for commercial, rental office, and car parking spaces.

Overseas Union Bank (OUB) Centre stands as one of the four tallest skyscrapers in Singapore. The tower is conceived to be two distinct volumes, a lower and higher tower, although structurally integral along with height changes. The slight space between the forms creates a sense of a shift in a once-whole form.

Both towers are triangular in plan and face each other on the hypotenuse. The taller one is supported by a service core and a triangular column in one corner. Imposed on the towers are square and circular designs that animate the exterior of the building. The facade is etched with a grid overlaid with larger rectangles, composed with smaller window units. These elements lead to a successful rhythmic effect.

The structure rises to 919 feet (280 meters) and contains 1.1 million square feet of office space. The steel frame allows for column-free floor space. The floor system consists of reinforced concrete slab composite with a ribbed steel deck. A major portion of the space below-grade is a reinforced concrete parking garage (to which a subway station is connected) and a shopping center. The exterior features a curtain wall of chemically treated aluminum alloy which changes color according to the light that it reflects.

The building entrance has a dramatic effect, tucked away into a 120-foot-high cutaway base which allows for a pleasant view of the surrounding area. Skylights and other lighting are used to create an airy feel to the public areas. The entire project cost around $150 million, and provides Singapore with a dramatic addition to its ever-changing skyline.

Overseas Union Bank Centre

Location: Singapore
Completion: 1986
Height: 919ft (280.1m)
Stories: 66
Area: 1.1 million ft²
Structure: Steel
Cladding: Aluminum
Use: Office

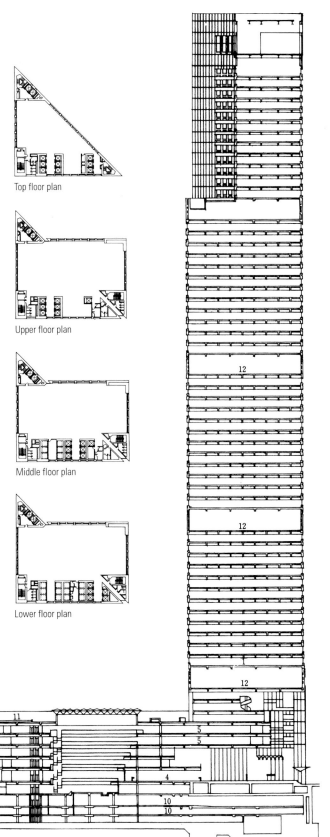

Top floor plan

Upper floor plan

Middle floor plan

Lower floor plan

2

3

4

1 Overseas Union Bank Centre (Opposite)
2 Section and floor plans
3 View from below
4 Skylights of the building entrance
Photography: Osamu Murai courtesy Kenzo Tange & Associates (1,3,4)

Architect: Kenzo Tange & Associates
Structural Engineer: W.L. Meinhardt
** & Partners Pty Ltd**
Services Engineer: Bylander Meinhardt Partnership
Project Manager: Overseas Union Project
** Management**
Developer: OUB Centre Limited

In the Raffles City complex, Republic Plaza joins the Overseas Union Bank and the United Overseas Bank as the latest tower to be built to Singapore's 919-foot height limit. Republic Plaza's styling defies the dated characterization of western skyscrapers, its design instead intending to invoke an 'oriental spirituality.' The tower becomes more slender as it rises with a succession of sloping facades. The transition from ground to sky is most evident in the skin of the building, which progresses from a granite base to a glass top. At night only the top of the tower which is lit from within is visible. Inside, the main lobby is a four-story space with polished granite and ceramic finishes. Fifteen double-decker elevators provide transportation. A bridge links the tower to the mass transit station across the street, and a 10-story garage is attached to the tower.

Republic Plaza was built in just under two years using the fast track process. The crowded city site is near an underground tunnel and several historic structures. Under the site natural boulders and abandoned piles from previous structures made construction of the foundation difficult. The contractor decided the answer was to construct the tower on a caisson with mini piles for additional support. More than 900 mini piles and a raft structure were used to support the building. The tower itself is framed by concrete-filled tubular steel columns. The floor beams and concrete floor slab make up the horizontal components of the hybrid structure which is a framework of high-yield structural steel beams. The project used 8,600 tons of structural steel and 31,000 cubic meters of concrete.

Lateral forces (wind and earthquake) are resisted by a combination of the core wall system with a moment-resisting frame on the exterior including outrigger braces.

The exterior finish is a combination of granite with strip windows and curtain wall made of tinted glass. The curtain wall surrounding the four sides is gradually inclined at the lower part of the building to smoothly shift the figure of the typical floor plan from the octagon at the upper part to the square at the lower part.

Republic Plaza

Location: Singapore
Completion: 1995
Height: 919ft (280.1m)
Stories: 66
Area: 1.3 million ft²
Structure: Mixed
Cladding: Granite, tinted glass
Use: Office

2

3

4

1   Republic Plaza (Opposite)
2   Raffles City
3   Entrance lobby
4   Street level
Photography: Masao Sudo courtesy Kisho Kurokawa
Architects & Associates (1,2); ©Shinkenchiku-sha Co. Ltd
courtesy Kisho Kurokawa Architects & Associates (3,4)

Architect: Kisho Kurokawa Architects & Associates
Associate Architect: RSP Architects Planners
& Engineers
Structural Engineer: RSP Architects Planners
& Engineers
Services Engineer: Squire Mech Pte Ltd
General Contractor: Shimizu Corporation
Developer: City Developments Limited

The United Overseas Bank Plaza (UOB) is located in the business center of Singapore next door to the OUB (Overseas Union Bank) Center that was built six years earlier by the same architect. The UOB Plaza actually consists of two office towers, the UOB at 66 floors and 919 feet (280 meters), the same as OUB, and a smaller high-rise at 38 floors.

The tower tapers at its top and is formed by square blocks nested to one another at 45 degree angles and sitting on an octagonal base. The articulation of the tower creates an outline that richly expresses the motion through the play of light and shadow. Each office within the multi-faceted tower gives a panoramic view, and provides an enjoyable space. The tower also contains a sky lobby located on the 37th and 38th floor, intended to provide a relaxing atmosphere for visitors.

The podium spans 45 meters and is supported by four large columns. It is the location for the banking hall and serves as the literal connection between the two towers. The podium is decorated with a 12-meter-high stainless steel tensile truss curtain wall located on the first floor of the banking hall. Visitors can walk directly through the banking hall from Raffles Place to the Singapore River. This space becomes an active and pleasant pedestrian area, while below an outdoor walkway provides access to the base of the towers.

During the construction of the smaller tower, built last in the complex, renovations were also made for the 66-story tower. The steel structural elements were untouched, but the interior, facades and equipment were renewed.

United Overseas Bank Plaza

Location: Singapore
Completion: 1992
Height: 919ft (280.1m)
Stories: 66
Area: 1 million ft²
Structure: Steel
Cladding: Granite
Use: Office

2

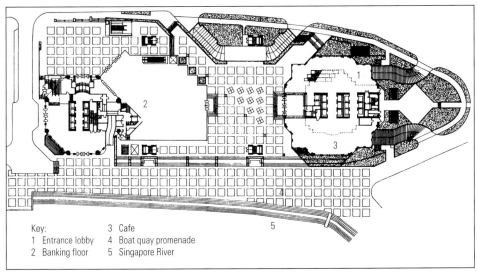

Key:
1 Entrance lobby
2 Banking floor
3 Cafe
4 Boat quay promenade
5 Singapore River

3

4

1 United Overseas Bank Plaza (Opposite)
2 Podium curtain wall
3 Site plan
4 Outdoor walkway
Photography: Osamu Murai courtesy Kenzo Tange & Associates (1,2,4)

Architect: Kenzo Tange & Associates
Structural Engineer: Ove Arup & Partners
Mechanical Engineer: J. Roger Preston & Partners
Developer: United Overseas Bank Ltd

Contractors: Nishimatsu Construction Co. Ltd
& Lum Chang Building Contractors

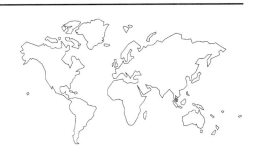

With its form outlined at night in argon gas lights and sheathed in silver reflective glass visible during the day, the 72-story NationsBank Plaza at Dallas Main Center dominates the Dallas skyline as its tallest building. Unlike many of the towers of the 60s and 70s that expressed their structure on the exterior, the owners of NationsBank wanted their tower free from any perimeter columns that would interfere with the view—which ruled out a tube. So an innovative structural system was developed which supported the gravity loads of the entire building (including the core) and resisted lateral forces.

As the result of a 'height pocket' in the Dallas zoning areas, NationsBank stands alone. West of the tower, building heights are limited by an historic area to under 100 feet, while to the east, the nearby airport limits buildings to 60 stories. The selection of the window color was a source of great debate, ranging from different colors to patterns. In the end, the more conservative silver reflective won because of its elegance of homogeneous design. On typical floors, the windows in this glass skin extend from 8 inches above the floor to the ceiling. The glazing is an energy-efficient insulated glass which, combined with the reflective coating, serves to cut cooling costs.

For interior design flexibility, NationsBank Plaza bucked the trend. The 16 major columns are located 20 feet from their centers to the exterior wall which allows for great flexibility in the arrangement of the exterior offices. Cantilevered off these concrete and steel columns are the exterior offices and the curtain wall, while the internal core is hung from a moment-resisting steel frame attached to the exterior columns. These steel frames act as Vierendeel trusses connecting the columns. Their unique 42-inch-deep size, not available in the United States, were made in Luxembourg. The core itself is cruciform in plan, allowing unobstructed access on each floor. The exterior columns support not only the gravity loads of the building but structurally resist the bending and shearing forces created by the wind, which is the greatest force which acts upon this building. The use of high-strength concrete saved more than $10 million. This structural system also allowed the building to be the slenderest tall building in the world at the time of construction, with a height-to-floor area ratio of 7 to 1.

NationsBank Plaza, an important force in revitalizing the historic west end of Dallas, features a sunken courtyard with landscaping, water, and public sculptures. The site also boasts connections to Dallas' underground walkway system, with a retail esplanade.

NationsBank Plaza

(Formerly: Interfirst Plaza)

Location: Dallas, Texas, USA
Completion: 1985
Height: 921ft (280.7m)
Stories: 72
Area: 2 million ft²
Structure: Mixed
Cladding: Glass
Use: Office

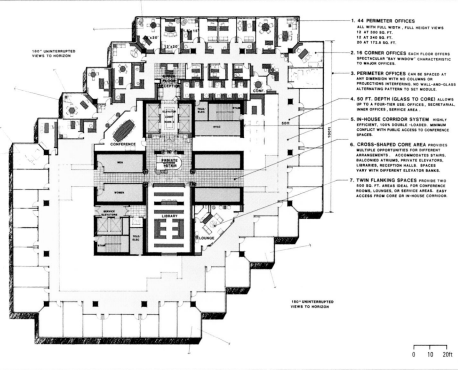

1. **44 PERIMETER OFFICES**
ALL WITH FULL WIDTH , FULL HEIGHT VIEWS
12 AT 300 SQ. FT.
12 AT 240 SQ. FT.
20 AT 172.5 SQ. FT.

2. **16 CORNER OFFICES** EACH FLOOR OFFERS
SPECTACULAR 'BAY WINDOW' CHARACTERISTIC
TO MAJOR OFFICES.

3. **PERIMETER OFFICES** CAN BE SPACED AT
ANY DIMENSION WITH NO COLUMNS OR
PROJECTIONS INTERFERING. NO WALL-AND-GLASS
ALTERNATING PATTERN TO SET MODULE.

4. **50 FT. DEPTH (GLASS TO CORE)** ALLOWS
UP TO A FOUR-TIER USE: OFFICES, SECRETARIAL,
INNER OFFICES , SERVICE AREA .

5. **IN-HOUSE CORRIDOR SYSTEM** HIGHLY
EFFICIENT, 100% DOUBLE -LOADED. MINIMUM
CONFLICT WITH PUBLIC ACCESS TO CONFERENCE
SPACES.

6. **CROSS-SHAPED CORE AREA** PROVIDES
MULTIPLE OPPORTUNITIES FOR DIFFERENT
ARRANGEMENTS . ACCOMODATES STAIRS,
BALCONIED ATRIUMS, PRIVATE ELEVATORS,
LIBRARIES, RECEPTION HALLS. SPACES
VARY WITH DIFFERENT ELEVATOR BANKS.

7. **TWIN FLANKING SPACES** PROVIDE TWO
500 SQ. FT. AREAS IDEAL FOR CONFERENCE
ROOMS, LOUNGES, OR SERVICE AREAS. EASY
ACCESS FROM CORE OR IN-HOUSE CORRIDOR.

180° UNINTERRUPTED
VIEWS TO HORIZON

180° UNINTERRUPTED
VIEWS TO HORIZON

0 10 20ft

2

3

4

1   NationsBank Plaza (Opposite)
2   Lit at night
3   Basic floor plan
4   Sculpture at entrance
Photography: R. Greg Hursley courtesy JPJ Architects (1,2,4)

Architect: JPJ Architects (Jarvis Putty Jarvis)
Structural Engineer: LeMessurier Associates
**Associate Structural Engineer: Brockette
    Davis Drake**
Services Engineer: Purdy McGuire Inc.
**Developers: Bramalea Texas, in association with
    Prudential Reality Group**
General Contractor: Austin Commercial

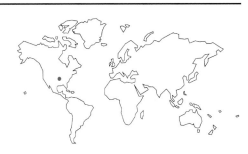

Located within the midblock between William Street and Broad Street and rising 927 feet in height is the 40 Wall Street building. Designed in 1928 and erected in record time of less than one year, it was built during a period in history when rivalry in the race to 'reach the sky' was at its most intense. The specific competition in 1928 was with the Chrysler Building, which had originally announced its height to be 925 feet. In fact the architect of 40 Wall Street, H. Craig Severance, was the former partner of William Van Alen, architect of the Chrysler Building. With new partner Yasuo Matsui, Severance set out to leapfrog Chrysler by adding an ornate pyramidal crown and a Gothic spire at 40 Wall Street, then known as Bank of Manhattan Trust. This massing of the new building took advantage of the setback regulation mandated by the zoning law passed in New York in 1916.

40 Wall Street was completed in May, 1930 at 927 feet. But Van Alen was not prepared to allow Severance to surpass him. So Van Alen added a 185-foot spire which, according to historians, was "secretly assembled within Chrysler's crown" and raised into place just as the tower was finished. At 1,046 feet, Chrysler thus tipped the balance in its favor, retaining the title briefly as the tallest building in the world, an honor soon ceded to the Empire State Building.

40 Wall Street continued to dominate the skyline of lower Manhattan however—but even that status lasted only two years. In 1932 the neighboring 952-foot American International Building at 70 Pine Street was constructed.

Irritated by Chrysler's victory, the architects of 40 Wall Street penned a newspaper article claiming that this tower was actually taller, since its observation deck, "the highest usable floor, was some 100 feet above Chrysler's," whose top spire was purely ornamental and effectively inaccessible. This deck—although very cramped—was open free of charge during business hours, up until World War II.

In 1996, Donald J. Trump announced a rehabilitation and conversion of this building, the "Crown Jewel of Wall Street" to its original grandeur, with "3,500 brand new Wausau windows, two 1,300-ton York chillers, state-of-the-art safety and telecommunication systems, and all new Italian marble and bronze lobby."

40 Wall Street

(Formerly: Bank of Manhattan Trust Building)

Location: New York, New York, USA
Completion: 1930
Latest Restoration: 1997
Height: 927ft (282.6m)
Stories: 72
Area: 903,000 ft²
Structure: Steel
Cladding: Italian marble
Use: Office

3

4

5

1 View of 40 Wall Street in the Manhattan skyline (Opposite)
2 Archways in the upper banking hall
3 Pyramidial crown
4 Ground floor elevator lobby
5 Banking hall on mezzanine level
Photography: courtesy The Trump Organization (2,4,5);
Douglas Mason (1,3)

2

**Architects: H. Craig Severance, in association with
   Yasuo Matsui**
Consulting Architect: Shreve and Lamb
Developer: Bank of Manhattan Trust Company
Owner: The Trump Organization

Columbia Seafirst Center is a six-sided tower with alternating straight sides and concave sides. As the building rises, two of the concave sides step back at the 43rd and 61st floor, to reveal the solitary partial ring, which rises to the top. In plan, the building can be described as three overlapping ring segments.

At the time of its completion, Columbia Seafirst Center was the tallest building in the United States, west of Mississippi. Originally designed as a 1,005-foot-tall tower, the FAA requested that the building be shortened because the building was in the flight path to the Seattle-Tacoma Airport. But the owner wanted the architect and engineer to retain the originally planned 76 stories of the tower. The design professionals met the challenge by shortening the floor-to-floor height from 12 feet to 11 feet 6 inches. These changes allowed the building to reach its 943-foot height and comply with the FAA requirements.

The excavation for the building's underground parking garage and foundation reached a depth of 135 feet and measured 240 x 248 feet, almost an entire city block, the largest such undertaking in the city up to that time. The tower is primarily a steel building. However, it is identified structurally as mixed construction because the main loads of the building are supported by three composite steel-and-concrete columns that measure 8 x 12 feet in plan. Constructed of clusters of wide flange columns embedded in concrete, these composite columns are located at the corners of the building core.

The core, 'a vertical bridge,' is constructed entirely of steel members of various shapes and sizes. Combined with the steel framing of the core, the composite columns resist wind and seismic forces while supporting the majority of the gravity loads of the building. Steel columns along the exterior perimeter of the building are spaced 16 feet on center around the building and support the balance of gravity loads. This framing system allowed for an amazingly low 14.8-pounds-per-square-foot of steel per floor.

The slender tower top of Columbia Seafirst Center could have been prone to an uncomfortable level of sway in severe wind storms, so dampers were added to the core. The dampers consist of a steel plate sandwiched between two steel Ts, connected by a rubberized plastic material.

The 4,000 people who work in the building and their visitors (up to 5,000 some days) are protected from fire by approximately 50,000 sprinklers. The building is serviced by 49 elevators, with speeds up to 1,200 feet per minute.

Columbia Seafirst Center

Location: Seattle, Washington, USA
Completion: 1984
Height: 943ft (287.4m)
Stories: 76
Area: 1.4 million ft²
Structure: Mixed
Cladding: Reflective glass
Use: Office

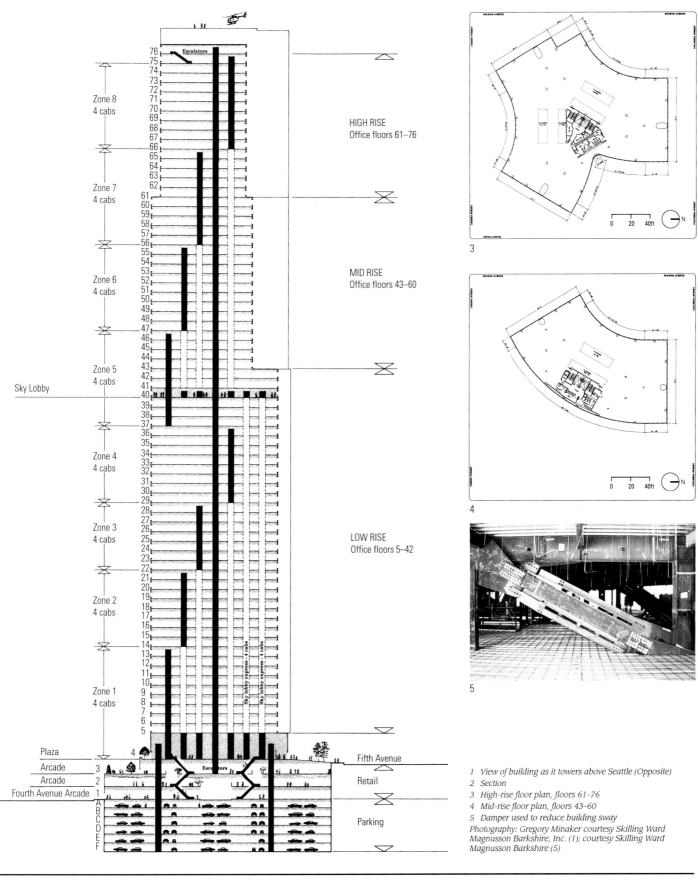

76
Escalators
75
74
73
72
71
70
69
68
67
66
65
64
63
62
61
60
59
58
57
56
55
54
53
52
51
50
49
48
47
46
45
44
43
42
41
40
39
38
37
36
35
34
33
32
31
30
29
28
27
26
25
24
23
22
21
20
19
18
17
16
15
14
13
12
11
10
9
8
7
6
5

Zone 8
4 cabs

Zone 7
4 cabs

Zone 6
4 cabs

Zone 5
4 cabs

Sky Lobby

Zone 4
4 cabs

Zone 3
4 cabs

Zone 2
4 cabs

Zone 1
4 cabs

HIGH RISE
Office floors 61–76

MID RISE
Office floors 43–60

LOW RISE
Office floors 5–42

Sky lobby express - 4 cabs
Sky lobby express - 4 cabs

Plaza   4
Arcade   3
Arcade   2
Fourth Avenue Arcade   1
A
B
C
D
E
F

Escalators

Fifth Avenue

Retail

Parking

2

3

4

5

1   View of building as it towers above Seattle (Opposite)
2   Section
3   High-rise floor plan, floors 61–76
4   Mid-rise floor plan, floors 43–60
5   Damper used to reduce building sway
Photography: Gregory Minaker courtesy Skilling Ward
Magnusson Barkshire, Inc. (1); courtesy Skilling Ward
Magnusson Barkshire (5)

Architect: Chester L. Lindsey Architects
Structural Engineer: Skilling Ward Magnusson
    Barkshire, Inc.
Mechanical Engineer: University Mechanical
Electrical Engineer: Cochran Electric
Developer: Martin Selig
General Contractor: Howard S. Wright Construction

If skyscrapers are an American architectural form, it is ironic that until 1987 Philadelphia's tall buildings were of modest height. While New York was completing the classical Chrysler and Empire State Buildings, the PSFS Building, the first international style skyscraper, was going up in Philadelphia. At 491 feet, it did not exceed the height of the City Hall's statue of William Penn, the city's founder. From that point on, a gentleman's agreement limited the height of buildings in Philadelphia to 491 feet. In 1983 a developer presented his plan to build the Liberty Place Towers several blocks west of City Hall on Market Street. On approval, his plan changed the skyline of Philadelphia forever. Recognizing many benefits for the city, the city council designated a special high-rise corridor along Market Street, where the view of William Penn was already obscured.

One Liberty Place is the tallest building among this new crop of skyscrapers within Philadelphia. The design approach of the architects towards One Liberty Place represents 'continuing efforts of striving toward a synthesis between the expression of the romantic yearnings of traditional skyscrapers and the display of modernist technological imagery.' One Liberty Place has been compared to the Chrysler Building, a welcome comparison, because of its slim shaft and gabled top.

The three-story podium with bay windows and granite finishes provides continuity and maintains the urban streetscape. The transition from the base to the shaft of the towers is evident in the change of the skin to a mixture of granite and glass. Vertical stone piers on the shaft emphasize the location of the structural columns. As the towers climb the granite diminishes until all that remains is the gabled glass. Inside, the multi-story lobby provides an elegant transition from the city street to the stacked office floors and links to the retail mall.

The structural system works like a sailboat mast, with the core acting as the mast and the exterior columns and outrigger connections acting as the support lines. The setbacks on the exterior emphasize the location of the eight major columns. These columns are tied to the four columns of the core with four-story steel outriggers, which are placed strategically throughout the building for greatest efficiency. 'This outrigger/supercolumn structure permits greater flexibility and openness for space and ground floor retail use than does the conventional 'tube system.'

For futher information regarding Liberty Place Complex, please see page 124.

One Liberty Place

Location: Philadelphia, Pennsylvania, USA
Completion: 1987
Height: 945ft (288m)
Stories: 61
Area: 1.2 million ft²
Structure: Steel
Cladding: Glass
Use: Office

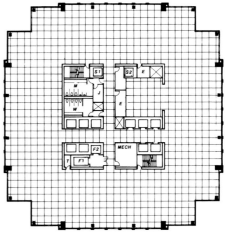

3

1 One Liberty Place (Opposite)
2 One Liberty Place at street level
3 Typical floor plan
4 One Liberty Place changed the skyline of Philadelphia
  forever
Photography: McGail and Williams courtesy Murphy/Jahn
Inc. Architects (2); McGail and Williams courtesy Murphy/
Jahn Inc. Architects (4)

2

4

Architect: Murphy/Jahn Inc. Architects
Structural Engineer: Lev Zetlin Associates, Inc.
Services Engineer: Flack & Kurtz
Developer: The Rouse Associates

S tone cladding, material changes, and surface treatments in the new building base reflect the scale and important lines of the original bank. Despite a physical connection, the perception will be of two polite yet independent urban neighbors.'

This was the architect's intent when the Society Tower was designed. The Tower, part of an urban redevelopment plan for the entire city block, is neighbor to the landmark Society for Savings Bank Building, designed by Burnham and Root in 1890. Permission to build Society Tower required Society Corporation to sell the Burnham and Root building to the Jacobs Group, as well as their headquarters elsewhere in the city, and agree to be major tenants of the new Tower. The Jacobs Group agreed to completely renovate the Burnham and Root building, which had fallen below life-safety standards. The renovation included restructuring the floor levels above the main banking hall to connect directly with the corresponding floor levels of the new Tower.

The completion of Society Tower in 1991 made it the tallest building in Cleveland. Set apart from its surroundings, it was designed so as not to overwhelm the original bank building. The Tower's 11-story base was set back with a wide reveal separating the two buildings. Although the original Society Bank Building and Society Tower are physically connected through the reveal, the Tower appears as an independent building. With a narrower face, the Tower is articulated in plan and section with several setbacks designed to create a sympathetic neighbor to the smaller bank building. The building is designed on the tripartite subdivision system. The base of the building is sheathed in a light-colored granite. The shaft of the Tower is articulated with vertical shafts of aluminum and glass with stainless steel framing. These vertical stripes give the Tower a thinner profile appropriate to the city and its skyline. The top culminates in a stainless steel crown.

The siting of the Tower in the center of Cleveland was designed as a visible landmark between Public Square and the Mall, the two main public spaces in downtown. Society Tower serves to reinforce the diagonal axis between the Mall and Public Square that culminates in the Terminal Tower. The Public Square is defined on three sides by the Terminal Tower, BP America Tower, and Society Tower. These three buildings serve to anchor the Public Square within the skyline of the city.

Society Tower

Location: Cleveland, Ohio, USA
Completion: 1991
Height: 950ft (289.6m)
Stories: 57
Area: 1.25 million ft²
Structure: Mixed
Cladding: Granite, aluminum, glass
Use: Office

2

3

4

5

1 Society Tower looking across plaza (Opposite)
2 Main banking chamber, old Society Bank Building
3 Lift lobby on east facade looking through to banking chamber
4 Carpets designed by Cesar Pelli in tenancy lift foyers
5 Looking at southwest corner showing historical old Society Bank Building
Photography: Tim Griffith courtesy The Images Publishing Group Pty Ltd

Architect: Cesar Pelli & Associates
Structural Engineer: Skilling Ward Magnusson Barkshire, Inc.
Services Engineer: Flack & Kurtz
Developer: Richard and David Jacobs Group

The First Canadian Place tower dominates the downtown Toronto area. The 72-story structure rises to 951 feet above the city, making it Canada's tallest building. The structure resembles a modified cruciform with a 15-foot indentation at each corner. This arrangement allows for eight corner offices per floor. The 3.5-million-square-foot tower takes up two acres of its seven-acre site, with the remaining five acres dedicated to public use. Surrounding the tower is a three-level podium creating an ideal space for shopping, entertainment, and recreational activities.

Italy's finest Carrara marble added to the beauty of both the tower and podium. The 72 floors of First Canadian Place each offer 30,000 square feet of column-free space, allowing for flexibility in floor planning. All windows are double-glazed, tinted, and heat-absorbing to eliminate heat and glare from the sun. At the same time, the windows reduce the noise from the hustle and bustle of downtown Toronto.

The tower is supported by a steel tubular frame. The structure consists of two tubes of vertical and horizontal steel, linked diagonally and horizontally. The inner tube typically surrounds the elevators and other core features, while the outer tube defines the external skin. Once the two tubes are linked, they work together to resist forces from wind and earthquakes.

The location and attractions of First Canadian Place draw thousands of people a day. Some 20,000 people work in the complex, and with 250,000 office workers within a half-mile radius of the complex, an estimated 30,000 people a day visit the complex. It is a vast network of walkways connecting the lower levels of major hotels, offices and transportation facilities covering a five-block area. The 36-foot sidewalk around the tower is designed to prevent congestion during the midday rush. Extensive landscaping and protected promenades surround the complex.

First Canadian Place achieves a balance between an office tower and recreational area for those who visit the financial district of Toronto. The complex represents both design technology and space efficiency as well as aesthetic appeal and convenience.

First Canadian Place

Location: Toronto, Canada
Completion: 1975
Height: 951ft (289.9m)
Stories: 72
Area: 3.5 million ft²
Structure: Steel
Cladding: Carrara marble
Use: Office

2

1   First Canadian Place (Opposite)
2   Outdoor plaza
3   Retail shops
4   Banking hall
5   Lobby
Photography: Fiona Spalding-Smith courtesy Bregman
+ Hamann Associates (1,2,3); Ian Leith (4); Michael Mitchell (5)

4

3

5

Architect: Bregmann + Hamann Associates
Structural Engineer: M.S. Yolles and Partners Ltd
Services Engineer: The ECE Group
Developer: Olympia & York/LMI

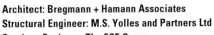

When completed in 1932, this building of 67 stories above ground and three below was the third tallest building in the world; all three were located in Manhattan. Today considered a 'landmark building,' it was the last of the great structures built in lower Manhattan before World War II. Its jazz-inspired Art Deco style colors the heart of the world's financial center—Wall Street.

The American International Building was erected by Cities Services Company, known today as CITGO. It is said that at one time the owner purchased another building on Wall Street, and built a bridge connecting his structure to the Wall Street building in order to gain the prestige carried by the Wall Street address. This connection was eventually torn down, however, and the building could no longer claim its '60 Wall Street' address.

It is in this skyscraper that double-decker Otis elevators were installed for the first time, one compartment serving the odd-numbered, the other even-numbered floors, both loading and unloading at the same time. This invention saved 24,000 square feet of floor space, a precious commodity at this highly valued location.

While the building foundations were being excavated for this tall and narrow tower, steel mills in the midwest United States operated around the clock to roll the 24,000 tons of beams and girders needed for its skeleton. As the skeleton began to rise, other materials followed from around the world—including dark gray Indiana limestone for the exterior trimming, eight million bricks for the tower shell enclosure, and miles of pipe and conduit wires and cables for its infrastructure. To decorate the elegant two-story lobby and the 66th-floor glass-enclosed observatory, other ornamental materials were shipped from France, Italy and Spain. Black and rose-tinted marbles for the floors and walls were shaped and polished in Minnesota and Tennessee. The American International Building was also among the first to make extensive use of aluminum on the exterior.

The 66th-floor observatory, perched high above the financial district, features a glass-enclosed solarium with terraces in all four directions and an inlaid compass in the polished stone floor. This elegant glass bubble, 'intimate and awe-inspiring,' is a private domain for executive employees of the American International Group, the owner of the building since 1976 and whose operations occupy most of the facility.

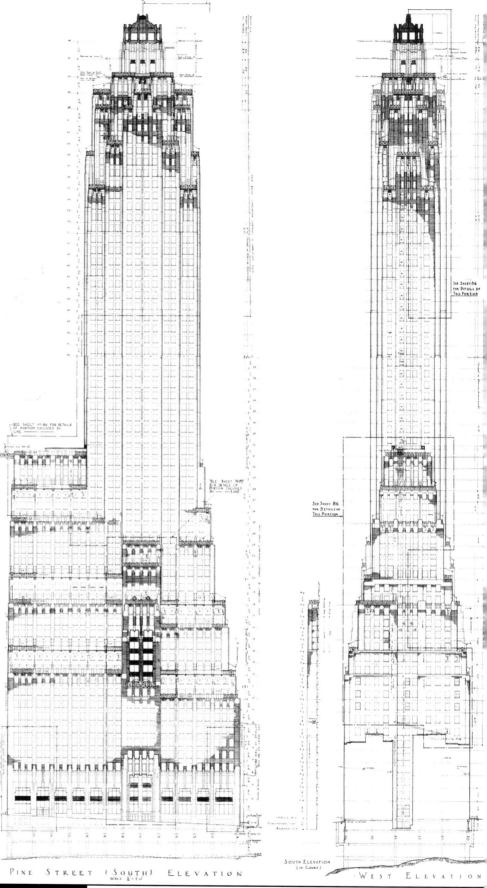

PINE STREET (SOUTH) ELEVATION

SOUTH ELEVATION (IN COURT)

WEST ELEVATION

American International Building (Formerly: Cities Services Building)

Location: New York, New York, USA
Completion: 1932
Height: 952ft (290.2m)
Stories: 67
Area: 865,000 ft²
Structure: Steel
Cladding: Indiana limestone, bricks, aluminum
Use: Office

2

3

1 Original blueprints showing elevations (Opposite)
2-4 Architectural details fill the building
5 Lift lobby
6 American International Building in the New York skyline
7 View of the American International Building
Photography: courtesy American International Realty Corp.

4

5

6

7

Architects: Clinton & Russell; Holton & George
Engineers: Taylor Fichter Steel Construction Inc.;
   Tenny & Dhems Inc. Consulting Engineers
Owner: American International Group
General Contractor: James Stewart & Co. Builders

Adjacent to Sears Tower is 311 South Wacker Drive, a 961-foot-tall tower that is the first phase of a three-tower development focused around a winter garden which serves as a pedestrian hub joining several transportation systems.

This 65-story office tower occupies an oversized city block of approximately three acres and contains 1.4 million-square-feet of office space. It is the sixth tallest building in Chicago after Sears, Amoco, John Hancock, AT&T, and Two Prudential Plaza, and the third tallest concrete frame building in the world at the time of construction.

One acre of the site is dedicated to a public space in the form of two large outdoor plazas. A covered pedestrian concourse traverses the site and a skylit 'winter garden' several stories high serves as a major public amenity. This winter garden or grand lobby also serves as a front door along Wacker Drive, providing a gracious transition between the tower and the street.

The massing of 311 South Wacker Drive is broken into a distinct series of elements, giving it legibility and scale and displaying its unique profile along the skyline on this western edge of the Loop. The architectural massing consists of a thick slab into which the octagonal tower is embedded. At the 51st-floor the octagon breaks free of its slab. These two massing elements, the slab and the octagonal tower, are joined together by horizontal strapping at the 5th, 13th, and 46th floors.

Above the 51st-floor the concrete column-and-beam framework is exposed, above which the tower terminates in a 70-foot-tall translucent glass cylinder. This cylinder is surrounded by four smaller glass cylinders, each of which is brightly lit at night, casting a glow in the Chicago skyline.

The facade of the lower floors of the building is dense and solid, covered in polished Amazon black and polished charcoal granite. Contrasting sections are of Verdi antique marble, which lock the light shaft into its base. A series of vibrant stone colors and textures along with intricate metalwork produce a rich tapestry at street level. The shaft of the building is sheathed in flame-finished Sunset Red granite, a light-color stone that sparkles in the sunlight and offers glittering contrast to its immediate neighbor, the Sears Tower. Silver reflective glass is set into silver aluminum frames throughout the building and stainless steel and white aluminum metalwork is used throughout.

311 South Wacker Drive

Location: Chicago, Illinois, USA
Completion: 1990
Height: 961ft (292.9m)
Stories: 65
Area: 1.4 million ft²
Structure: Concrete
Cladding: Granite
Use: Office

1   Model (Opposite)
2   View of building
3   311 South Wacker Drive under construction, Sears Tower
    is on the left
4   Bird's-eye view
5   Tower lobby floor plan
6   Typical floor plans 14–46
Photography: courtesy Kohn Pedersen Fox Associates (1,2);
Ivan Zaknic (3,4)

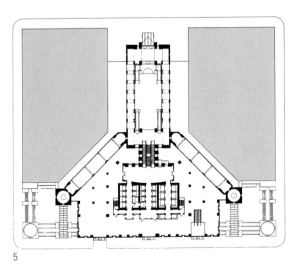

2

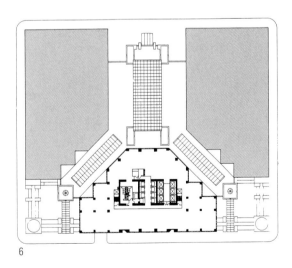

4

5

6

Architects: Kohn Pedersen Fox Associates
   with Harwood K. Smith & Partners
Structural Engineers: Brockette & Associates,
   with C.P. Stefanos Associates
Services Engineer: Brady, Lohrman & Pendelton Inc.
Developers: Lincoln Property Company and Teachers
   Insurance and Annuity Associates

Owner: Lincoln Properties
General Contractors: J.A. Jones
   Construction Company with
   Harbour Construction Company

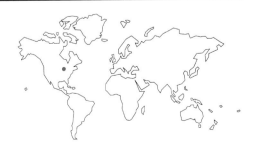

Located in the virtual center of downtown Houston, First Interstate Bank Plaza rises above the cement and metal boxes which surround it. Besides its sheer height, First Interstate Bank Plaza distinguishes itself through its subtle design—two quarter circles set slightly apart, sheathed in blue-green reflective glass. The floor plan and glass curtain wall rise up, without setbacks, to the full height of the building, in direct contrast to its neighbor First International Plaza.

The architects designed First Interstate Bank Plaza and its neighbors to work together to complement one another. Nowhere is this more evident than on ground level, where public plazas connect all these buildings. These public plazas are an amenity few buildings offer in downtown Houston because of the city's small 250-foot-square blocks. The tower offers a unique entrance which serves as a gateway to the building and an entrance to the climate-controlled underground tunnel system. This portico is encased in a marble cube frame which graces the bridge from street level into the lobby of the building. On either side of this bridge are stairs to the underground tunnel system.

First Interstate Bank Plaza would appear to be one of the few buildings in Houston in which concern is expressed for the human scale of the building and its effects on the inhabitants of the city. This is evident not only through its emphasis on making the entrance a rich experience, but also through subtle features on the glass curtain wall which sheathes the building. To break up this large expanse of glass and the overall massing of the building, the structure was expressed through the vertical and horizontal mullions. Whereas the main grid is dark green, the tracks for the window-washing equipment are stainless steel.

The purpose of the special exterior design was to enhance and unify downtown Houston, with an interior designed to be as flexible as possible for the tenants. With almost 25,000 gross square feet available on each floor and all the structure located along the wall and in the central elevator core, the needed flexibility was achieved.

The structure was conceived as a bundled tube design. With columns along the exterior curtain wall located 15 feet on center, the design proved so effective structurally that no additional interior columns or bracing in the core was necessary. This core space was minimized through the use of double-decker express elevators running to two separate 'sky lobbies,' which serve the three main vertical divisions throughout the building.

1

2

First Interstate Bank Plaza

(Formerly: Allied Bank Plaza)

Location: Houston, Texas, USA
Completion: 1983
Height: 972ft (296.3m)
Stories: 71
Area: 1.8 million ft²
Structure: Steel
Cladding: Glass
Use: Office

3

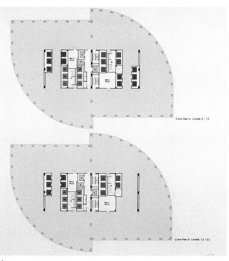

4

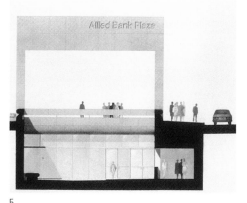

5

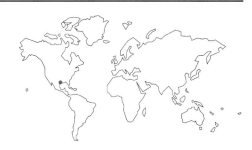

1 First Interstate Bank Plaza rises majestically above
   its neighbors (Opposite)
2 First Interstate Bank Plaza reflects its surroundings
   (Opposite)
3 Ground level view
4 Typical floor plan
5 Cutaway view of street level and lower level of First
   Interstate Bank Plaza

*Photography: Hedrich-Blessing courtesy Skidmore,
Owings & Merrill (1,2,3)*

Architect: Skidmore, Owings & Merrill (SOM)
Associate Architect: Lloyd James Brewer
**   & Associates**
Structural Engineer: SOM
Services Engineer: I.A. Naman
Developer: Century Development Corporation
General Contractor: Miner-Turner

The Landmark Tower in Yokohama, Japan is a mixed-use structure that rises to a height of 971 feet and 70 stories, making it the tallest building in Japan. In plan, the Tower is designed as a square with projecting corners that slope inward as they rise.

The Tower's tapered form is clad in granite and contains 1.5 million square feet of office space on 52 floors. A hotel occupies the upper 15 floors, with 500,000 square feet of usable space. The top two floors have two restaurants and an observation deck looking out toward Mt. Fuji or to the Pacific Ocean. A skylit swimming pool and health facilities are located at the base of the hotel portion of the Tower.

The Tower is only part of the much larger mixed-use complex. The 10-acre site, which is bounded by elevated moving sidewalks from Sakuragi-cho Station, has a Grand Mall located near the base of the Tower. This retail block also accommodates hotel facilities such as lobby, banquet, and reception rooms. Three levels of parking are located underground.

Structurally, Landmark Tower is a tube within a tube. A composite system is used up to the ninth-floor to increase lateral stiffness, boost compression strength, and add mass to resist overturning. The steel-framed tubes on the upper floors are tied together with braces. Two tuned active dampers are located at the 282 meter level, each equipped with a tuned spring system and a control system so they can act in two directions.

Landmark Tower, in addition to being the tallest in Japan, holds the Guiness Book of World Records for the fastest elevator installed in a building: 41 feet a second.

This building synthesizes oriental simplicity with modern technology and has become the symbol of redevelopment by the municipal government in Japan.

Landmark Tower

Location: Yokohama, Japan
Completion: 1993
Height: 972ft (296.3m)
Stories: 70
Area: 4.2 million ft²
Structure: Steel
Cladding: Granite
Use: Multiple

2

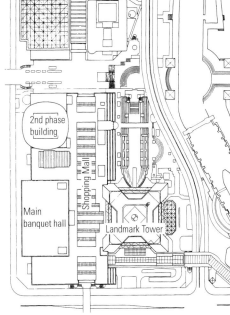

3

4

5

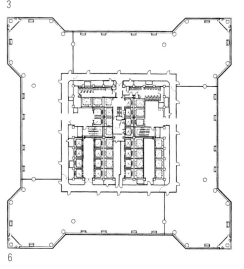

6

1   View from the east (Opposite)
2   Dockyard garden in the evening, a launching point for
    cultural activities
3   Site plan
4   Landmark Plaza brings greenery indoors
5   Shopping at Yokohama's waterfront in Landmark Tower
6   Floor plan
Photography: Akisi Miwa courtesy Mitsubishi Estate Co., Ltd
(1); Kousi Miwa courtesy Mitsubishi Estate Co., Ltd (4,5)

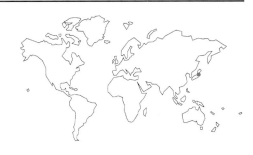

**Architects: Stubbins Associates and Mitsubishi
    Estate Co., Ltd**
Structural Engineer: Le Messurier Consultants Inc
Services Engineer: Syska & Hennessy
Developer: Mitsubishi Estate Co., Ltd
**Principal Construction Firms: Taisei Corporation
    and Shimizu Corporation**

With the approaching new millennium, the Commerzbank Headquarters provides us a glimpse of the future. The holistic design of the building incorporates economics, architecture, engineering, and urban planning, with concerns for the environment and the health of the users.

The combination of three 52-foot-deep x 131-foot-wide towers into a triangular tower with a central atrium, allows the tower to achieve its great height. The tallest building in Europe, it is one of the few buildings in Germany to utilize steel as the primary structural material. Every three stories of the tower consist of two office wings linked by a three-story skygarden. At the corners of each side are structural columns which support the tower as well as other core elements standard to each floor. Attached to the columns are vierendeel trusses which support each floor and skygarden, while allowing column-free interior spaces and a rational exterior skin free from diagonal bracing. These steel elements created a simple kit of parts which increased prefabrication off-site and simplified on-site connections.

By German law all office workers must be within 7.5 meters of a window, which set the 16 meter (52-foot) depth of each office wing. The skygardens and triangular central atrium allow light to pass to the interior faces of each wing, while also encouraging interaction between personnel. Transparent ceilings of glass and steel at various levels in the atrium reduce strong updrafts. All windows are a two-piece unit with a fixed outer skin which acts as a windscreen with ventilation slots at top and bottom and an inner skin with a tilting pane. The office workers have manual control of their windows, while a computer-controlled weather-monitoring system operates the windows in the public spaces and overrides the manual controls in the event of inclement weather. The columns in the core act as chimneys, drawing out warm air from the offices during the day. At night the concrete floors draw in cool air. These passive designs diminish the energy costs of the structure associated with the air conditioning and heating systems. The low energy use of the building created by this combination of features afforded the owners a special permit to increase the height of the building over what would otherwise have been permitted.

Commerzbank Headquarters

Location: Frankfurt, Germany
Completion: 1997
Height: 981ft (299m)
Stories: 56
Area: 1.3 million ft²
Structure: Mixed
Cladding: Aluminium, glass
Use: Office

2

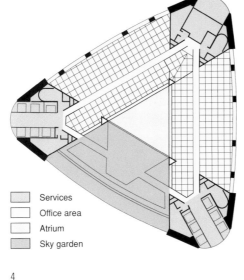

Services
Office area
Atrium
Sky garden

4

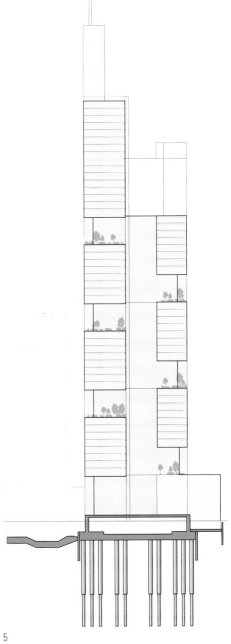

5

3

1 Commerzbank Headquarters (Opposite)
2 Commerzbank Headquarters provides office workers with
   a view of the interior atrium
3 Interior view
4 Typical floor plan
5 Cross-section
Photography: Ian Lambot courtesy Ove Arup & Partners
(1,2,3)

Architect: Sir Norman Foster & Partners
Structural Engineer: Ove Arup & Partners
Associate Structural Engineer: Krebs & Keifer
Mechanical Engineer: J. Rogers Preston
Associate Mechanical Engineer: P & A Petterson
  Ahrens

Electrical Engineer: Schad & Holzel
Developer: Commerzbank
General Contractor: Hochtief AG

This distinctive 64-story structure, clad in two shades of gray granite and reflective glass, is part of the Prudential Plaza redevelopment project. This includes One Prudential Plaza, a renovated 41-story tower built in 1955, a new public plaza and a five-level underground parking garage that accommodates 500 cars. It is situated at the center of a major underground walkway system connecting directly to the Illinois Central Railroad. An exterior arcade creates a new base at the lower three stories with a colonnade wrapped around both the existing and the new towers, joining the two tall buildings.

Two Prudential Plaza soars 920 feet (280m) to the beginning of its 75-foot spire, making it also the world's fourth-tallest concrete skyscraper at 995 feet (303m). Prudential requested that this new tower be designed to recall One Prudential Plaza in color and vertical expression. The building's north and south facades display gable-shaped recesses with skylights at the 42nd and 52nd floors. The new one-acre terraced and landscaped plaza, featuring two fountains, waterfalls and flowers, provides an inviting outdoor setting for tenants, visitors, and passers-by.

Floor plans range from 22,500 square feet at the low-rise portion of the building to 15,500 square feet in the high-rise portion, reflecting the building's geometry of multiple cantilevered corners providing prime office space with corner offices.

Concrete was chosen because of its scheduling and economic advantages, ease of installation of the granite skin, and above all for its rigidity. In this windy city, the limiting-sway requirement (nine inches at the top of a structure) could be achieved only through the use of high-strength concrete with superplasticizers. This high-strength concrete also diminished the size of the columns, thus allowing more rentable floor space with fewer columns, and provided natural fireproofing, one of the great advantages of concrete.

The building's shape at the top, with its succession of layered chevrons in its graceful transition from the shaft to the spire, has been widely compared to the Chrysler Building. Two Prudential Plaza has added to the quality of life and attractiveness of the downtown Chicago area.

Two Prudential Plaza

Location: Chicago, Illinois, USA
Completion: 1990
Height: 995ft (303.3m)
Stories: 64
Area: 1.2 million ft²
Structure: Concrete
Cladding: Gray granite, reflective glass
Use: Office

3

2

4

1 *Two Prudential Plaza (Opposite)*
2 *Plaza in the evening*
3 *Entranceway*
4 *Fountain at entrance*
Photography: Mark Ballogg ©Steinkamp/Ballogg Chicago
courtesy Loebl Schlossman and Hackl Inc. (1); Wayne Cable
courtesy Lobel Schlossman and Hackl Inc. (2); George Lambros
courtesy Loebl Schlossman and Hackl Inc. (3,4)

Architects: Loebl, Schlossman & Hackl Inc.
Structural Engineer: CBM Engineers Inc.
Services Engineer: Environmental System
    Design Inc.
Developer: The Prudential Property Company
General Contractor: Turner Construction Company
Project Manager: Garrison Associates Inc.

Upon completion in 1982, the 1,000-foot-high Texas Commerce Tower in Houston, became the tallest building outside Chicago and New York, the sixth tallest building in the nation, and the tallest composite building in the world.

Clad in pale gray polished granite, stainless steel and gray glass, the 75-story Tower departs from the classic four-sided box building design with one corner sheared at a 45 degree angle to produce a five-sided structure. The front facade is an 85-foot column-free span of butt-jointed glass and stainless steel spandrels running the entire height of the Tower.

Rising from a 62,500-square-foot site, the Tower is set on one corner of the site, forming an open L-shaped plaza on another corner. The plaza is paved with rose and gray flamed granite and bordered on each side with landscaped gardens. Its focal point is a bronze and steel sculpture, 'Personage with Birds.'

The plaza's paving extends into the five-story main lobby and is repeated in the 13-foot-high sky lobby on the 60th floor. Both lobbies have interior walls of polished gray granite. The ground floor lobby has curved balconies with stainless steel rails over granite parapets at four levels. A tapestry called 'Six Flags over Texas' hangs on the wall in the banking hall on the first level. Typical office floors start on the third level and the building contains over 1.3 million net square feet of space.

Below ground level, the concourse has piers clad with polished gray granite, inset with glass fronts. Granite paving extends from the circulation areas around the retail and restaurant facilities (27,000 square feet) and into access points to the tunnel system connecting the buildings within the central business district. Parking for 192 cars is located on two levels below the concourse.

The structural steel, which precedes the concrete work in a composite building such as Texas Commerce, limited access for handling formwork, as well as placing the concrete. The resulting custom-built jump form system eliminated the need for a crane, and pumped cast-in-place concrete was used for construction. The Tower received three major awards for pumping concrete more than 1,000 feet high. A record-setter at the time of construction in 1981, the 1,007-foot pumping height was a full 40% greater than the previous height record of 729 feet set in 1980.

Texas Commerce Tower

(Also known as: United Energy Plaza)

Location: Houston, Texas, USA
Completion: 1982
Height: 1,000ft (304.8m)
Stories: 75
Area: 1.3 million ft²
Structure: Mixed
Cladding: Gray granite
Use: Office

1 Texas Commerce Tower (Opposite)
2 Sculpture by Joan Miro
3 Gray granite plaza
4 Banking Hall displaying the 'six flags of Texas'
5 Lobby
Photography: Richard Payne courtesy Pei Cobb Freed &
Partners (1,3,5); Nathaniel Lieberman courtesy Pei Cobb
Freed & Partners (2); Hedrich-Blessing courtesy Pei Cobb
Freed & Partners (4)

3

4

5

Architect: I.M. Pei & Partners
Associate Architect: 3D/International Architects
Structural Engineer: CBM Engineers Inc.
Services Engineer: I.A. Naman Associates, Inc.
Developers: Gerald D. Hines Interests & Texas
**   Commerce Bank**
General Contractor: Turner Construction Company
Artist - Sculpture (Plaza): Joan Miro
Artist - Tapestry (Banking Hall): Helena Hernmarck

This 60-story, 1.7 million-square-foot tower is located in the heart of the new center of business activity and expanding development in Chicago. The designers attempted to make a connection to the tradition of the great American skyscraper in Chicago's skyline, including the Palmolive Building, the Carbide and Carbon, the Chicago Board of Trade, and the Field (now La Salle National Bank) Building. And although the building takes full advantage of state-of-the-art structural and mechanical systems, expressing its modernism architecturally through the extensive use of glass, its massing is a strong reminder of the optimistic spirit of the American skyscraper of the earlier epoch.

The tower sits upon a highly articulated five-story granite base with bronze-accented entries and storefronts, reinforcing the building's vital connection to the urban and commercial fabric of the Loop, and providing a generous amount of retail space and a friendly dialogue with the pedestrian. The building changes color as it rises from deep red at the ground floor to a lighter red facing between the second and the fifth floor, to a lighter rose for the tower above. Recessed spandrels and accent pieces are a deep green granite with a decorative abstract pattern.

At the 30th, 45th and 49th floors there is a five-foot setback reinforcing the termination of elevator banks, while a special setback at the 15th floor refers to the prevailing building line of Chicago's early skyscrapers, all of them defining a strong silhouette against the skyline.

The lobby spaces of the ground floor are designed as a series of grand-scale rooms finished in oak and a variegated palette of marbles. The main three-story lobby off Monroe Street, 48 feet high, follows the tradition of European great halls, rich in detailing and the use of elegant marbles, gold leaf, bronze and oak wood trim. Three custom-made chandeliers illuminate the lobby, which leads to a five-story atrium at mid-block, opening onto the Franklin Street lobby.

Similar motifs of the main lobby are reflected in the two ground floor elevator lobbies, as well as in the 'skylobbies' on the 29th and 44th floors, featuring 1930s Art Deco details on the walls, floor, and lighting. In the escalator lobby, the architects provided four large oculi, or circular windows, cut into the walls which are tongue-in-cheek references to a similar motif of the famous AT&T parent building in New York. The top of the building is crowned by four spires embellished with fins and open metalwork, gently tapering as they rise 130 feet above the rooftop.

The AT&T Corporate Center office tower, at a cost of $600 million, was designed with energy efficiency in mind, with a computer-controlled HVAC system and environmentally designed exterior walls. The client took the lead in addressing social concerns by initiating an aggressive and unprecedented affirmative action program in hiring contractors and subcontractors for the project and making the complex fully handicapped accessible.

AT&T Corporate Center

Location: Chicago, Illinois, USA
Completion: 1989
Height: 1,007ft (306.9m)
Stories: 60
Area: 1.7 million ft²
Structure: Mixed
Cladding: Granite
Use: Office

3

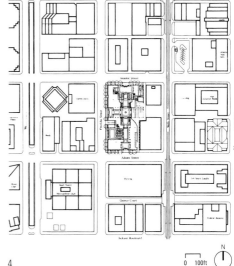

4

1 AT&T Corporate Center (Opposite)
2 Three-story lobby in the European tradition
3 Decorative lighting adds a special touch
4 Site plan
Photography: courtesy Skidmore, Owings & Merrill (1,2);
Ivan Zaknic (3)

2

Architect: Skidmore, Owings & Merrill (SOM)
Structural Engineer: SOM
Developer: Stein & Company
Owners: AT&T, Stein Partnership

General Contractors: Mayfair Construction;
  Blount Brothers
Project Manager: Mike Oppenheim Assoc.
Lighting Consultant: Jules, Fisher & Paul Marantz

First Interstate World Center came into being in 1990, in part because of its neighbor, the 1926 Los Angeles Central Library. Gutted by fire in 1986, the library was slated for the wrecking ball—until the sale of its air rights to First Interstate World Center. The sale enabled the Library to be restored and modernized, and enabled First Interstate World Center to rise to its present height of 75 stories.

In designing First Interstate World Center, the architects deferred to the Library in design. The tower's base and shaft are simplified with very little ornament. The top of the tower, however, is sheathed in a multi-faceted glass crown, which is illuminated after dark.

Located just 26 miles from the San Andreas fault, the structure of the building was designed to withstand an earthquake the magnitude of 8.3 on the Richter scale. The structure needed to be not only flexible enough to absorb the forces of an earthquake, but also stiff enough to resist the enormous wind forces on a building of this height. A moment-resisting steel frame on the exterior perimeter of the tower (designed for ductility against seismic loading) and a rigid 74-square-foot steel core extend the full height of the building, together providing lateral support against the load. First Interstate World Center is the tallest building in the world in an earthquake Zone 4.

The tower is organized by a simple geometry of an overlapped circle and square, with the circle emerging beneath the crown as the dominant geometrical form. The curved colonnade of structural piers at street level, each encased in translucent envelopes of green tinted glass, serves a variety of functions. The sweeping curve softens the impact of the enormous structure on the site, allowing the building at ground level to defer to the Library across the street. The colonnade creates a feeling of transparency and openness at grade-level, welcoming the passers-by. These articulations provide the tower with a subtle privacy at street level, while the setbacks in the facade and distinctive crown create a memorable image for the building in the city's skyline.

Another element on the site is the Bunker Hill Steps, a monumental stairway with a fountain and cascading waterway. The steps serve as a pedestrian link between the tower and the office and retail complexes nearby.

Great buildings become symbols of their city. First Interstate World Center's ascendancy into the central point of Los Angeles was marked in 1997 by its 'destruction.' Destruction, that is, in the film 'Independence Day'—the first building in the movie to be targeted by the alien space invaders.

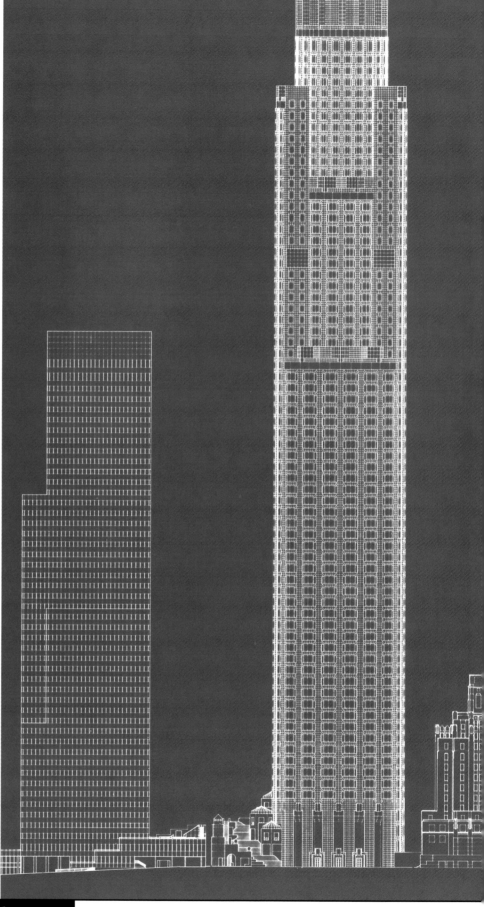

First Interstate World Center

(Formerly: Library Tower)

Location: Los Angeles, California, USA
Completion: 1990
Height: 1,018ft (310.3m)
Stories: 75
Area: 1.5 million ft²
Structure: Mixed
Cladding: Granite, glass
Use: Multiple

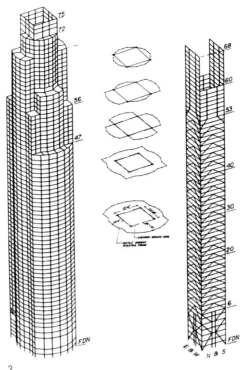

2

3

1   Fifth Street elevation (Opposite)
2   View of First Interstate World Center
3   Building section
4   First Interstate World Center in the Los Angeles' skyline
    Photography: Jane Lidz courtesy Pei Cobb Freed & Partners

4

Architect: I.M. Pei & Partners
Services Engineer: James Knowles and Associates
Structural Engineer: CBM Engineers
Developers: Maguire/Thomas Partners with Pacific Library Tower
Owner: Maguire/Thomas Partners
Contractor: Turner Construction Co.

In midtown Atlanta, between Peachtree and West Peachtree, stands one of the many skyscrapers that give the city its spectacular skyline. Its 1,023-foot-height makes it the tallest in Atlanta providing a signature unmistakable from other skylines.

The building comprises 1.35 million gross square feet, with 1.27 million square feet of usable office space. The tower has a three-level wing attached at the base, containing a bank branch, which opens onto the lobby. One can also find inside a restaurant, retail shop, conference center, and health club. Reflective glass covers the north wall, visually enlarging the outside environment. The tower consists entirely of office space, with parking provided on four decks below ground level.

The form of the tower is emphatically vertical, with carefully proportioned, uninterrupted lines running the length of the shaft. Notched corners step back at the 41st and 52nd levels. Forty-foot arched entries are flanked by 70-foot granite piers which appear to anchor the building to the ground. The red granite and gray-tinted glass curtain wall covers the exterior.

The tower is square in plan and is rotated 45 degrees on the site, which provides undisturbed views in all directions. It also provides northern or southern exposures for almost all offices in the building. The tower is flanked on either side by landscaped parks. Pedestrians can walk through the parks and enter directly into the tower lobby. They can also approach the building through a mirrored-glass gallery from the mass-transit stop located opposite one corner of the site.

The tower uses a super-column structural scheme. Two large columns, eight feet square at the base, are located at each tower face and at each corner of the central core. They act as both vertical support and wind bracing. This system eliminates costly interior columns and provides maximum office space and design flexibility.

Above the sleek vertical tower is a stepped pyramidal cage formed by closely spaced horizontal tubes. This pyramid encloses the cooling tower, elevator penthouses, and other mechanical equipment. It is, in turn, surmounted by a 90-foot fiberglass spire that pierces the sky. At night, the pyramid is illuminated from the interior, adding a softly-glowing beacon to the Atlanta skyline.

NationsBank Plaza

Location: Atlanta, Georgia, USA
Completion: 1993
Height: 1,023ft (311.8m)
Stories: 55
Area: 1.27 million ft²
Structure: Mixed
Cladding: Granite, glass
Use: Multiple

2

4

1 At night, the NationsBank Plaza cap glows in the Atlanta sky (Opposite)
2 Lobby
3 Arched entry
4 Elegant hallway
Photography: courtesy Kevin Roche John Dinkeloo and Associates (1,2,3,4)

3

Architect: Kevin Roche John Dinkeloo and Associates
Structural Engineer: CBM Engineers, Inc.
Services Engineer: Environmental Systems Design
Developer: Gerald D. Hines Interests
General Contractor: Beers Construction Company

The Chrysler Building is recognized as New York City's greatest display of Art Deco magnificence. Automobile tycoon W.P. Chrysler bought the 39,456 square-foot-site on which the 77-story office building would be erected. Construction began in October, 1928 and was completed in May, 1930.

At the time of its completion the Chrysler Building was one of the world's most ornate office buildings and the world's tallest structure, at a height of 1,046 feet. Four months later the championship would be claimed by the Empire State Building.

The importance of accessibility and transit facilities was reflected in its location across the street from Grand Central Station, and the building's conveniences and facilities resulted in the satisfaction of the business man.

Lobby walls three stories high rise from the ground level and are the first prominent display of the Art Deco interior and facade. Its walls and floor are covered in materials from around the world: a dark green Norwegian granite 'proscenium-like' entrance, blue marble from Belgium, red marble from Morocco, and Sienna travertine from Germany. The ceiling mural, one of the largest ever designed, depicts a view of the Chrysler Building, several airplanes of the period, and scenes from the assembly line at the Chrysler automobile plants.

The four elevator banks contain 30 passenger elevators, of which no two are alike. Each elevator door displays a modernistic use of wood veneer on steel. The interiors are faced with a wide variety of woods: Japanese ash, American walnut, Oriental walnut, English gray hardwood, dye ebonized wood, and curly maple.

Above the 30th level, the facade's Art Deco style is strongly exemplified by a frieze of hubcaps with protrusions of steel and mudguards. The tower's corners at this level have protruding steel decorations of winged radiator caps. Just above the 60th level, there are four corners with steel American eagle gargoyles.

At the 72nd level six stainless steel arcs begin, for which 20,961 tons of structural steel were used. Each arc, one surmounted by another, is complemented with triangular windows. The overall effect is one of 'six shimmering sunbursts, all culminating in a stainless steel needlepoint spire.' The spire alone adds 187 feet to the height. The actual materials used in the arc and spire structures are platinum-colored, non-magnetic, non-tarnishing Nirosta chrome-nickel steel which was bolted onto wooden forms.

Chrysler Building

Location: New York, New York, USA
Completion: 1930
Height: 1,046ft (318.2m)
Stories: 77
Area: 1.04 million ft²
Structure: Steel
Cladding: Brick
Use: Office

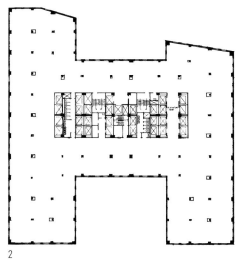

2

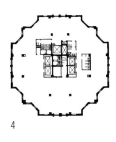

3

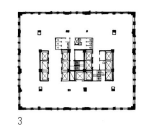

4

5

6

7

1   Chrysler Building lights up the New York sky
    (Opposite)
2-4 Typical floor plans
5   Elevator door
6   Entrance
7   View of Art Deco spire
Photography: courtesy Chrysler Properties Inc. and
Cushman and Wakefield (1); Douglas Mason (5,6,7)

Architect: William Van Alen
Structural Engineer: Ralph Squire & Sons
Services Engineer: Louis TM Ralston
Developer: W.P. Chrysler
Owner: Tishman Speyer Properties
Contractor: Fred T. Ley and Co. Inc.

The John Hancock Center, affectionately known as 'Big John,' is located on North Michigan Avenue along Chicago's 'Magnificent Mile.' With 100 floors, it accommodates office and residential, shopping and parking, with a public observation platform on the 94th floor, and a panoramic restaurant on the 95th and 96th floors. Instead of constructing a separate 45-story apartment tower and 70-story office building, which would have occupied most of the site and interfered with privacy and daylight, the two functions were combined into one tower of 100 stories. Offices occupy the lower floors and apartments are on the upper. Only 50% of the site is actually covered by the building, leaving the rest as open space.

The 711 apartments within this building range from efficiencies to four-bedroom luxury residences. Additional facilities include restaurants, health clubs, a swimming pool, and an ice skating rink: in effect, a small vertical city-within-a-city. At the top of this 1,127-foot building is a transmitter for some of Chicago's major television stations.

Fifty elevators and five escalators carry 12,000 passengers a day. Because of its multiple functions, John Hancock Center stimulates desirable inner-city vitality even after sunset.

In order to reach its height of 1,127 feet above ground, this colossal tower of 384 million pounds was designed to rest on large caissons that extend down to bedrock. One of the caissons reached 191 feet below ground—the deepest ever sunk in Chicago. For this job, the most powerful drilling rig ever devised was built.

The tapering shaft rises from 40,000 square feet at the base to an 18,000-square-foot summit. This tapered form provides structural stability as well as space efficiency. The exterior columns and spandrel beams create a steel tube that is reinforced by the clearly articulated diagonal bracing and structural floors that meet those diagonals and corner columns. The overall result is a very simple and highly efficient structural system.

The innovative structure is also quite economical, since it required only half the steel that would have been needed for a building with traditional interior columns (29.7 pounds-per-square-foot of floor area vs 45 to 50). The steel structure is clad in black aluminum accented with tinted bronze glare-reducing glass and bronze-colored aluminum window frames. The base of the building and lobbies are clad in travertine marble.

John Hancock Center

Location: Chicago, Illinois, USA
Completion: 1969
Height: 1,127ft (343.5m)
Stories: 100
Area: 2.8 million ft²
Structure: Steel
Cladding: Black aluminum, glass
Use: Multiple

2

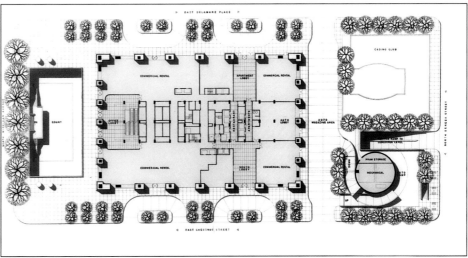

1 John Hancock Center rises above its neighbors (Opposite)
2 Bracing
3 Observation deck
4 Articulated diagonal bracing
5 Site Plan
Photography: George Hunter courtesy Skidmore, Owings
& Merrill (1); Ivan Zaknic (2,3,4)

3

4

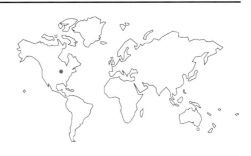

5

Architect: Skidmore, Owings & Merrill (SOM)
Structural Engineer: SOM
Services Engineer: SOM
Developer: John Hancock Mutual Life Insurance
   Company

Consultants: Paul Weidlinger and Ammann
   & Whitney
General Contractor: Tishman Realty
   & Construction Co
Steel Fabricator: Allied Structural Steel
Steel Erector: American Bridge Division of US Steel
   Corporation

This pristine tower is square in plan, measuring 194 feet on each side with 15-foot cut-outs at the four corners. Each floor plate covers approximately 30,700 square feet. The slender steel structure was originally clad in white Carrara marble, with its strong vertical emphasis making it seem even taller.

Until the completion of the Sears Tower in 1974, the Amoco Building (then known as Standard Oil) was Chicago's tallest building and the world's tallest marble-clad structure. The building occupies only 25% of its site. The tower design is based on an innovative tubular structural system, in which closely-spaced peripheral columns form a hollow tube. Five-foot 'V'-shaped sections, part of the building frame, absorb wind loads. The system permits a column-free interior and totally flexible floor planning between the service core and the exterior walls.

The perimeter of 'V'-shaped steel columns also house the piping and utility lines, eliminating the need for interior column chases that so often rob buildings of valuable office space. Double-decker elevator cabs serving the building also conserve office footage by minimizing shaft space in the building. Single-decker elevators service the lower levels. The north and south lobbies are illuminated by 11-foot-high custom-designed crystal chandeliers, each weighing 3,000 pounds. Cost to construct the building was $120 million.

The building underwent extensive renovation from 1990-1992 when its marble veneer required total replacement. Due to its high sensitivity to heat and cold the original Italian marble panels had bowed into warped dish shapes caused by uneven expansion. Twenty years after it was built, the one-and-one-quarter inch thick Carrara marble facing (the same marble used by sculptor Michelangelo) was replaced by two-inch-thick Mt Airy granite panels. All 43,000 panels were replaced on the building at the cost of about $80 million.

Part of the redevelopment also included the upper and lower plaza areas, and a new two-story arched vestibule serving as a main entrance to the building. The upper plaza combines a landscaped sitting area with garden sculptures. The lower plaza features a 197-foot-long waterfall and sunken garden which can function as a stage for various theatrical and musical performances.

The building's other amenities include a full-service 25,000-square-foot cafeteria for breakfast and lunch and five additional eateries in the retail lobby. There is also a full-service US Post Office, a bank, retail shops, meeting facilities including a 243-seat auditorium, and an athletic club. An underground four-level parking facility accommodates 679 cars.

Amoco Building

(Formerly: Standard Oil Building)

Location: Chicago, Illinois, USA
Completion: 1973
Height: 1,136ft (346.3m)
Stories: 80
Area: 2.7 million ft²
Structure: Steel
Cladding: Mt Airy granite
Use: Office

2

3

4

5

1 Amoco Building (Opposite)
2 The Plaza is a favorite gathering place
3 Arched entrance
4 Careful landscaping at street level
5 Waterfall
Photography: Hedrich-Blessing courtesy
The Amoco Corporation

Architects: Edward Durrell Stone and Associates, in association with The Perkins & Will Partnership
Structural Engineer: The Perkins & Will Partnership
Developer: Standard Oil Company of Indiana
Owner: Standard Oil Company of Indiana
General Contractor: Turner Construction Company

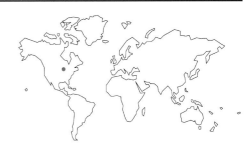

When the Bank of China building was being planned, there were special nuances connected with its development. The architect, a Chinese-American whose father once worked for the Bank of China, designed it with the bamboo shoot in mind— 'advancing with every stage of growth.' The building was topped out on the 8th day of the 8th month in 1988—the luckiest day of the Century, according to the Chinese. Indeed, the Bank of China has been acclaimed for its unusual geometric design, likened to a "glittering tower of diamonds," says its structural engineer.

Unofficial preliminary reports suggested that the design did not take into account the *Feng Shui* tradition in Hong Kong. *Feng Shui* is the ancient Chinese art of evaluating buildings to determine how the building will fit within the cosmic balance. The sharp geometry of the building would slice the delicate *yin yang* balance of the world and direct the cosmic anger of its sharp points towards the building's neighbors. However the art of *Feng Shui* is not recognized by the Chinese government so the building was built as designed.

When the Bank of China was completed, it was the tallest building in Asia at 1,209 feet. For the first time, a mega-structure composed of a pure space-truss was used to support the weight of a skyscraper, and the Bank of China made full use of the system to resist the strong typhoon winds of Hong Kong.

The Bank of China was engineered on principle described by the structural engineer as follows: "A single eccentricity in a column will cause bending; but two or more lines of eccentricity, joined by a uniform shear force mechanism, will counteract and therefore eliminate the bending. The five composite columns of the system support the braced frame of structural steel that spans them. The centroid, shape, and position of these columns change as they move down the building—the source of eccentricity. But because the concrete 'glues' the steel to itself, bending is eliminated."

The base of the building is sheathed in light granite which allowed the base to seem rooted in the ground. It also allowed for shaping and sculpting with the landscape, and did not clash with the aluminum and glass curtain wall of the tower.

The entrances to the Bank of China are on two different levels, so a combination of escalators and elevators transport users to their destinations. The base is a traditional square tube. Going up the building, the square, dividing into four triangles, begins to drop quadrants— the first triangle at the 25th-floor, the second at the 38th-floor, and the third at the 51st-floor. The Bank of China crests in a 55-foot-high atrium which rises a total of 17 of the 70 stories of the building.

Bank of China

Location: Hong Kong
Completion: 1989
Height: 1,209ft (368.5m)
Stories: 70
Area: 438,864 ft²
Structure: Mixed
Cladding: Aluminum and glass
Use: Office

3

4

2

5

**Architects: I.M. Pei and Partners in association with
   Wong/Kung & Lee**
Structural Engineer: Robertson Fowler & Associates
**Associated Structural Engineer: Meinhardt
   Hong Kong**
**Services Engineers: Jaros Baum & Bolles,
   with Associated Consulting**
Developer: Bank of China

This reinforced concrete office complex, rising 78 stories with three levels below ground, was both the tallest building in Asia and the world's tallest reinforced concrete building at the time of its construction.

The site was acquired at a government auction in 1989, at a price of $430 million for the land alone—establishing a record for the highest priced piece of real estate in Hong Kong.

Situated opposite Hong Kong's Convention Center, this building is triangular in plan with notched corners. A floor area of 24,000 square feet makes it one of the largest in Hong Kong. Given its column-free rentable areas, it allows for maximum flexibility in layout and high efficiency for its tenants. It was estimated that $30 million was saved by choosing reinforced concrete for its structure which, although it reduces the height of the structure, increases the floor plate area from 18,000 square feet to 24,000 square feet. Its total construction cost was $141 million.

This triangular and monumental pillar is capped by a pyramidal roof above which the mast is placed, shining when flood–lit at night.

Central Plaza's tower stands on a 100-foot-high podium block. The tower itself consists of three sections: first the base or the podium forming the main entrance and public circulation spaces; then the tall tower consisting of 57 office floors, a skylobby at the 46th-floor; and the tower top consisting of six mechanical plant floors culminating at the 75th-floor, crowned by a three-legged mast at the three truncated corners. The apparent triangular shape is not truly triangular because all three corners are cut off. This is for two reasons: first, to provide more appropriate internal space; but most importantly to avoid possible offence to its neighbors by directing its sharp triangular points at them. This would be considered not only impolite, but bad *Feng Shui*, an important consideration in this part of the world.

The facade is clad in insulated glass of three different colors. Gold and silver coating is used in a vertical and horizontal pattern and is juxtaposed with a ceramic painted pattern glass to create the classical and shimmery image.

The ground-floor level has a beautiful large landscaped garden which complements its adjoining public sitting area forming together a garden dedicated for public enjoyment and facilitating a pedestrian thoroughfare at the center of a very busy commercial district.

Central Plaza

Location: Hong Kong
Completion: 1992
Height: 1,227ft (374m)
Stories: 78
Area: 1.86 million ft²
Structure: Concrete
Cladding: Insulated ceramic plated glass
Use: Office

2

3

4

5

6

1   Central plaza glimmers in the sun (Opposite)
2   Sunset in the Hong Kong skyline
3   Central Plaza
4&5   Level 75 observation gallery
6   At night
Photography: Colin Wade courtesy Ove Arup & Partners (1–6)

Architects: Ng Chun Man & Associates, Architects and Engineers, and Dennis Lau
Structural Engineer: Ove Arup & Partners (Hong Kong)
Services Engineer: Associated Consulting Engineers
Developers: Sun Huang Kai Properties, Sino Land Co. Ltd, Ryoden Property Development Co. Ltd

The Empire State Building, built between 1930–31, remained for 41 years the tallest building in the world. In 1972, the World Trade Center towers claimed this distinction—but did not replace the Empire State Building's symbolic association with New York City. Even today, the Empire State remains an internationally known landmark and probably the most famous building ever erected, attracting five million visitors from all over the world each year.

The Empire State has been billed as the 'Eighth Wonder of the World,' and has often been used as a backdrop for movie companies. In 1933 it was the scene of a celebrated battle, as King Kong clung to the top of the building, grabbing at bi-planes that were shooting at him. Not all the drama has been staged, however. On a foggy Saturday morning in July 1945, a B-52 bomber on the way to Newark Airport crashed into the 79th floor. The building suffered only minor damage.

During planning and construction, the design changed 16 times but the construction was completed in just over one and a half years. Three thousand workers were on the job daily; the building set the record at the time for speed of construction. In addition to 60,000 tons of steel, the building was finished with 200,000 cubic feet of Indiana limestone and granite, 10 million bricks, and 730 tons of aluminum and stainless steel.

The main shaft of the building rises 85 floors above the setbacks that were required by the New York City 1916 Zoning Law (first at 73 feet, next at 250 feet). This profile has been copied around the world.

The structure is a standard riveted steel frame with simple portal bracing. The girders are riveted throughout their depth to the columns and beams. The facade is of granite, with chrome-nickel chips and Indiana limestone with mullions of stainless steel. The three-story lobby, considered a true work-of-art, is covered in marbles from France, Germany, and Belgium—at times construction emptying the contents of an entire quarry.

The lighting atop the Empire State Building has changed throughout the years. The first light to shine was a searchlight beacon which proclaimed the election of Franklin D. Roosevelt as President in 1932. In 1956, revolving synchronized beacons called 'Freedom Lights' were installed, and could be seen from as far away as 300 miles. Today colored lights celebrate holidays and other events year-round with various lighting combinations.

Empire State Building

Location: New York, New York, USA
Completion: 1931
Height: 1,250ft (381m)
Stories: 102
Area: 2.2 million ft²
Structure: Steel
Cladding: Indiana limestone, granite, brick
Use: Office

2

3

4

5

6

7

1 Under construction (Opposite)
2 Empire State Building majestically rises above other buildings in the New York skyline
3 Interior detail
4 Plaque to honour trades
5 Main entrance
6 Main lobby detail
7 Observation deck plaque
Photography: courtesy Empire State Building (1);
Douglas Mason (2,3,4,5,6,7)

Architects: Richmond Shreve, William Lamb and Arthur Harmon
Structural Engineer: H.G. Balcom
Developer: John Jacob Raskob
Contractor: Starrett Brothers and Ekin

At the time of their completion in 1972 and 1973, these two Towers were the tallest buildings in the world: 1,368 feet for the first Tower; 1,362 feet for the second. But only two years later it was the Sears Tower in Chicago that assumed the coveted title of the World's Tallest Building at 1,450 feet. The near-twin Towers continue to dominate the lower Manhattan waterfront however, and provide an impressive gateway to New York, with the Statue of Liberty in the bay nearby.

The architects created an outstanding example of Modernist architecture in a Neo-Gothic revival style, with floor-to-ceiling windows and delicate arch-like tracery at ground level. Some critics have even considered the Towers to be 'Neo-Classical'—due perhaps, to the interior lobbies, which run six stories high and are finished with highly polished Regina di Bianchi marble, stainless steel, and crystal chandeliers.

Built on six acres of landfill, the foundations extend 70 feet below ground to rest on solid bedrock. Around the foundation site, a long 'bathtub' had to be created to prevent seepage from the Hudson River.

The Towers were, for their time, the best-known example of a 'framed tube.' The closely spaced exterior columns and beams form a steel tube which, together with the internal frame, made it possible to withstand not only all the gravity loads but even more critically the wind loads that would be expected for these very tall buildings in this location. The framed tube transfers all load down to the buildings' foundations. At the very top, the maximum wind drift is just three feet. The construction involved extensive use of steel (192,000 tons) and an unparalleled amount of glass (a ribbon of glass, twenty inches wide, would run 65 miles). Each tower has 23 shuttle elevators.

On Friday, February 26, 1993 at 12:18 pm, a 22-foot-wide, five-story deep crater was blown into the lower level of One World Trade Center by an exploding bomb. 50,000 people were stranded in darkness and confusion. Six were killed and more than 1,000 injured.

Three thousand people worked for two weeks around the clock, merely to clean up the debris. Time was of the essence, for the Port Authority was losing $1 million a day in rent. The Towers were cleaned, repaired, and reopened between March 18 and April 17, 1993.

World Trade Center Towers

Location: New York, New York, USA
Completion: 1972 (One World Trade Center)
1973 (Two World Trade Center)
Height: 1,368ft (417m) (One World Trade Center)
1,362ft (415.1m) (Two World Trade Center)
Stories: 110 (Both Towers)
Area: 13 million ft² (Both Towers)

Structure: Steel
Cladding: Aluminium, steel
Use: Office

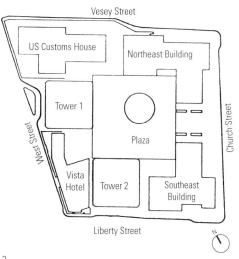

Vesey Street

US Customs House

Northeast Building

West Street

Tower 1

Plaza

Church Street

Vista Hotel

Tower 2

Southeast Building

Liberty Street

N

2

3

1　Detail of exterior (Opposite)
2　Plaza sculpture
3　Site plan
4　Windows light up the ground floor entrances
5　The towers are the tallest in the Manhattan Skyline
6　View from ground level
Photography: courtesy The Port Authority of New York and New Jersey (1); Ivan Žaknic (2); Douglas Mason (4); The Port Authority of New York and New Jersey (5,6)

4

5

6

Architect: Minoru Yamasaki and Associates
Associate Architect: Emery Roth & Sons
Landscape Architect: Sasaki, Dawson, and Demay
Structural Engineer: Skilling, Helle, Christiansen, Robertson
Mechanical Engineers: Jaros, Baum & Bolles

Developer: The Port Authority of New York and New Jersey
General Contractors: Tishman Realty and Construction Corporation
Interior Designer: Arcop Associates, Forb and Earle

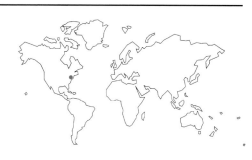

The design of the Jin Mao Building recalls the ancient pagoda forms of China, gently stepping back to create rhythmic patterns as it rises upward. According to its designer, this is a 'Sino-Art-Deco' building, based on multiples of the figure eight, considered a lucky number in the Chinese tradition. Its metallic forms change as the sun moves across the articulated surfaces, and at night the tower and its top are illuminated, a beacon on the Shanghai skyline.

The tallest building in China and the fourth tallest in the world, the tower is located in the Pudong district of the Lujiazui Finance and Trade Zone of Shanghai. This multi-use complex consists of an 88-story tower and a 6-story podium building, comprising offices, hotel, and retail commercial.

Office space occupies the 3rd–50th levels of the tower, and a five-star Grand Hyatt Hotel fills the top 38 floors, with spectacular views of the surrounding region for its 555 rooms. The podium contains hotel-related areas, a conference and exhibition center, a cinema auditorium, and a retail galleria.

The base of the tower is surrounded by a landscaped courtyard with a reflecting pool. An undulating glass clearstory and skylight provide a lively shopping experience. From the main boulevard to the north, the shopping atrium is distinguished by a special curved glass wall. Additional retail space is located at the second level, including a post office, courier service, a travel office, and customs department.

Below grade, the complex has three levels accommodating 993 cars and 1,000 bicycles, hotel service facilities, retail space, a food court, an observatory entry lobby, electrical transformers, a sewage treatment plant, a domestic water plant and a boiler and chiller plant.

The site conditions were difficult—sandy soil with no bedrock within 100 meters (328ft). The area is also prone to typhoons and earthquakes, additional factors which influenced structural design. The structural engineer devised a protective structure in reinforced concrete around the central portion, then went up with a combination of high-strength concrete and structural steel. Above grade, a reinforced concrete core and eight perimeter supercolumns are linked by outrigger trusses to resist lateral and vertical loads. Below the frame of the building a 4-meter reinforced concrete mat with 429 hollow steel piles extend 65 meters into the sand and clay soil. Although this stiff sand provides some bearing capacity, the building's primary support depends on pile friction.

Jin Mao Building

Location: Shanghai, People's Republic of China
Completion: 1998
Height: 1,380ft (420.6m)
Stories: 88
Area: 3 million ft²
Structure: Mixed
Cladding: Reflective glass
Use: Multiple

2

3

1 Model of Jin Mao Building (Opposite)
2 Rendering of 88th-floor Skydeck Observatory
3 Window wall
4 Rendering of entry way to retail stores in podium building
Photography: James R. Steinkamp courtesy Steinkamp/
Ballogg (1); Peter Weismantle courtesy Skidmore,
Owings & Merrill (3)

4

Architect: Skidmore, Owings & Merrill (SOM)
Structural Engineer: SOM
Services Engineer: SOM
Developer: China Shanghai Foreign Trade Company,
    Ltd (CSFTC)

Owner: CSFTC
General Contractor: Shanghai Construction Group
    Consortium

For 22 years, Sears Tower was the champion as the tallest building in the world. Still the tallest building in the western hemisphere, it boasts the tallest occupiable floor and the tallest skyscraper roof in the world. It is also the largest private office building in the world with some 3.7 million square feet of office space. 'Form Follows Function' is the only way to describe the Sears Tower.

The Sears Tower is the quintessential example of the revolutionary bundled-tube structural system, providing Sears with large, virtually column-free spaces and 70-foot clear spans. As the building climbs upward, the tubes begin to drop off, and the wind forces on the building are reduced. The square tubes measure 75 feet x 75 feet with perimeter columns spaced at 15 feet on center. At the base, nine tubes rise to the 49th-floor. Two tubes drop off at the 50th and at the 66th floors and three at the 90th-floor, allowing the last two tubes to rise to the building's 110-story top. To reduce shear stress, the structure has diagonal bracing only on the two levels (mechanical floors) before each setback. The 222,500-ton building is supported by 114 caissons that reach bedrock.

The exterior skin of the building is an expression of the structural skeleton inside, with the fireproof frame sheathed in black aluminum and glare-reducing bronze-tinted glass. The exterior skin of the Sears Tower is maintained with yearly check-ups and six window-washing machines.

In 1985, renovations to the lobby and the commercial levels were completed which added a separate entrance for tourists. A mobile car/elevator by Alexander Calder was installed in the existing lobby. Underground commercial spaces feature shops, a health club and restaurants. The exterior plaza has planters and benches, and is provided with underground heating elements to melt snow and ice. Two antennae on the roof provide services for over 20 television stations. Cameras on the roof monitor traffic below for commuters. On a clear day tourists look out from the 106th-floor at four states and over 200 points of interest. The tower contains enough concrete to build an eight-lane highway five miles long; 76,000 tons of steel, enough to build 50,000 automobiles; and enough telephone wiring to wrap around the world 1.75 times. Computer-controlled monitors continually adjust heat and light levels to keep energy costs low and comfort levels high.

Sears Tower

Location: Chicago, Illinois, USA
Completion: 1974
Height: 1,450ft (442m)
Stories: 110
Area: 3.7 million ft²
Structure: Steel
Cladding: Black duranodic aluminum
Use: Office

2

Plan shapes

3

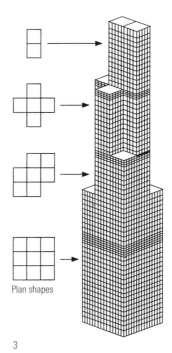

4

5

1 Sears Tower (Opposite)
2 Atrium lobby
3 Modular floor configuration
4 Lobby stairway
5 Atrium entrance
Photography: Tim Hursley (1); Ivan Zaknic (2); Skidmore, Owings & Merrill (4,5)

Architect: Skidmore, Owings & Merrill (SOM)
Structural Engineer: SOM
Service Engineer: Jaros, Baum & Bolles
Owner/Developer: Sears Roebuck and Company
General Contractor: Diesel Construction

Interior Space Planners: Saphier, Lerner, Schindler, Inc.
Skydeck Entrance Design: DeStafano & Partners

For the first time ever, the tallest building in the world is located outside the United States. Actually the record-holder consists of two identical structures rising 1,483 feet on the site of a former race track in Kuala Lumpur, the capital city of Malaysia.

Part of the 14-acre Kuala Lumpur City Centre (KLCC) development, the Towers contain more than 8 million square feet of office space, 1.5 million square feet of retail and entertainment facilities, underground parking for 4,500 cars, a petroleum museum, a symphony hall, and a multi-media conference center.

A unique feature of the 88-story Towers is the skybridge at the 42-story level. The bridge, with its angled support, creates what the architect calls 'a portal to the sky,' appearing as a monumental gateway.

The profile of the two Towers is unique in its floor template as well as its graceful silhouette. Its plan consists of two rotated and superimposed squares connected by small circular infills, which could be interpreted as Islamic in inspiration, and at the same time remain clearly modern and western. The buildings are clad in stainless steel and not the mirror glass that is common to so many other buildings in this tropical region.

These two supertall Towers are framed by a 152-foot-diameter concrete perimeter tube, connected by floor diaphragms consisting of composite metal decks on 18-inch-deep rolled steel beams to a high-strength reinforced concrete core measuring 74.8 x 75.4 feet. The core columns are connected at the corners to the perimeter tube by four reinforced concrete Vierendeel trusses at the 38th-floor above ground.

The Tower foundations consist of a raft and four-foot by nine-foot rectangular friction piles, called barrette piles, up to 340 feet in length. These piles do not reach bedrock. The structural loads above are carried by 16 concrete columns placed where the figures (circular and square) intersect.

The principal occupant is Petronas, the national petroleum company owned by the Malaysian government. The offices and malls of the KLCC are expected to attract an average of 50,000 people a day, a problem which has been handled through a light rail transit station, underground passageways, and widening an access road.

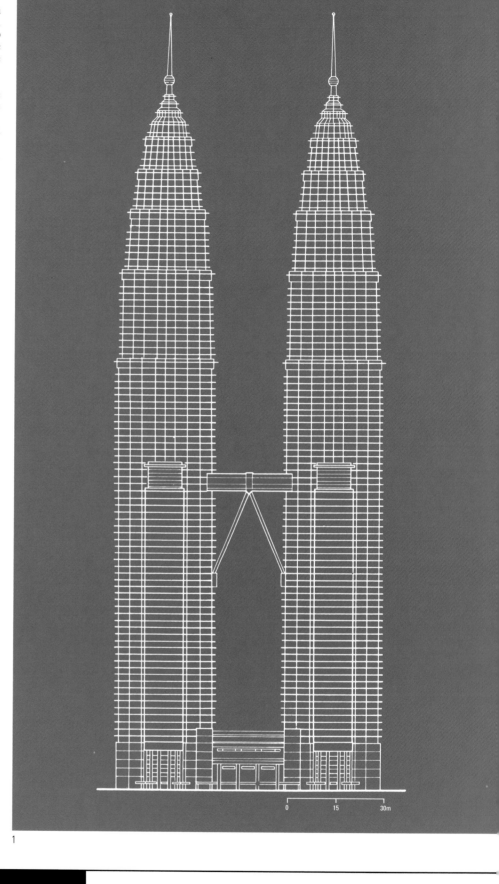

1

Petronas Towers

Location: Kuala Lumpur, Malaysia
Completion: 1998
Height: 1,483ft (452m)
Stories: 88
Area: 9.5 million ft²
Structure: Mixed
Cladding: Aluminum, stainless steel
Use: Multiple

2

3

4

5

6

1 Elevation of Petronas Towers (Opposite)
2 Pinnacle
3 Viewpoint of a pedestrian
4 Aerial view of project site
5 Tower top drawing
6 Skybridge
Photography: J. Apicella courtesy Cesar Pelli & Associates

Architect: Cesar Pelli & Associates
Associate Architects: RSP Architects Planners,
Adamson Associates and Studios
Structural Engineers: Thornton-Tomasetti and
Ranhill Bersekutu
Services Engineers: Tenaga Ewbank Preece
and Flack and Kurtz
Developer: Kuala Lumpur City Centre Corporation

Owner: Petronas
Project Manager: Lehrer-McGovern

Ten Tall Buildings Under Construction

Graha Kuningan

Location: Jakarta, Indonesia
Scheduled for Completion: 1998
Height: 784ft (240m)
Stories: 52
Area: 1.6 million ft²
Structure: Mixed
Cladding: Metal, glass
Use: Multiple

Architects: NBBJ; Ellerbe Beckett
Structural Engineer: Leslie E. Robertson Associates
Services Engineer: Meco Systech
Developer: Pacific Metro Realty
Photography: Paul Davis and Peter Pran courtesy NBBJ, Ellerbe Becket and PMR

BDNI Center - Tower B

Location: Jakarta, Indonesia
Scheduled for Completion: 1999
Height: 788ft (240.2m)
Stories: 45
Area: 757,000 ft²
Structure: Mixed
Cladding: Curtain wall, metal, glass
Use: Office

Architect: Pei Partnership
Structural Engineer: Leslie E. Robertson Associates
Services Engineer: Jaros, Baum & Bolles
Developer: Sentra BDNI Development
Photography: © Jock Pottle/Esto courtesy Leslie E. Robertson Associates

JR Central Towers

Location: Nagoya, Japan
Scheduled for Completion: 1999
Height: 820ft (249.9m)
Stories: 59
Area: 4.4 million ft²
Structure: Mixed
Cladding: Granite, stainless steel, concrete, ceramic tile
Use: Multiple

Architects: Kohn Pedersen Fox Associates PC
  and Sakakura Architectural Institute
Structural Engineer: Taisei Corporation
Services Engineer: Taisei Corporation
Developer: Central Japan Railway Co. Ltd
Photography: © Jock Pottle/Esto courtesy Kohn Pedersen Fox Associates PC

Tianjin World Trade Center

Location: Tianjin, China
Scheduled for Completion: 1999
Height: 853ft (260m)
Stories: 64
Area: 2 million ft²
Structure: Steel
Cladding: Curtain wall, granite
Use: Multiple

Architects: JWDA and Tianjin Building Design Institute
Structural Engineer: Martin & Huang International
Services Engineer: Martin & Huang International
Developers: Holland O'Kawa Group and He Hua Real
  Estate Development Co. Ltd
Photography: courtesy Martin & Huang International

Nanjing Xi Lu

Location: Shanghai, China
Scheduled for Completion: 1998
Height: 923ft (281.3m)
Stories: 62
Area: 3.2 million ft²
Structure: Mixed
Cladding: Stainless steel, granite, silver aluminum, glass
Use: Office and retail

Architect: Kohn Pedersen Fox Associates PC
Structural Engineer: Thornton-Tomasetti Engineers
Services Engineer: Flack & Kurtz Consulting Engineers
Developer: Hang Lung Development Company, Ltd
Construction Manager: Shanghai Construction Group
  Consortium CBSO
Photography: Jock Pottle/Esto courtesy Kohn Pedersen Fox Associates PC

The Centre (Queen's Road Central)

Location: Hong Kong
Scheduled for Completion: 1998
Height: 958ft (292m)
Stories: 73
Area: 1.5 million ft²
Structure: Steel
Use: Multiple

Architect: Dennis Lau and Ng Chan Man & Associates
Structural Engineer: Maunsell Consultants Asia Ltd
Services Engineer: Flack & Kurtz Consulting Engineers
Developer: Cheung Kong Ltd and Land
    Development Corp.
Construction Manager: Paul Y-ITC Construction Ltd
Photography: courtesy Maunsell Consultants Asia Ltd

Telekom Malaysia Headquarters

Location: Kuala Lumpur, Malaysia
Scheduled for Completion: 1998
Height: 1,017ft (310m)
Stories: 55
Area: 1.6 million ft²
Structure: Concrete
Cladding: Concrete, glass
Use: Office

Architect: Hijjas Kasturi Associates Sdn
Structural Engineer: Ranhill Bersekutu
Services Engineer: Zainuddin Nair & Ven Associates
Developer: Telekon Malaysia Berhad
Photography: courtesy Hijjas Kasturi Associates Sdn

Plaza Rakyat

Location: Kuala Lumpur, Malaysia
Scheduled for Completion: 1998
Height: 1,254ft (382.2m)
Stories: 77
Area: 1 million ft²
Structure: Mixed
Cladding: Stainless steel, glass, metal panels, concrete
Use: Multiple

Architect: Skidmore, Owings & Merrill (SOM)
Structural Engineer: SOM
Services Engineer: SOM
Developer: Daewoo Corporation
Photography: Steinkamp Ballogg courtesy Skidmore,
Owings & Merrill

Shanghai World Financial Center

Location: Shanghai, China
Scheduled for Completion: 2001
Height: 1,509ft (459.9m)
Stories: 95
Area: 1.04 million ft²
Structure: Mixed
Cladding: Metal, glass
Use: Office

Architects: Kohn Pedersen Fox Associates PC;
    Mori Building Architects and Engineers Co.;
    East China Architectural Design and Research Institute
Structural Engineer: Ove Arup & Partners
Services Engineer: Shimizu Corporation
Developer: Forest Overseas Co. Ltd
Photography: Edge Media courtesy Kohn Pedersen Fox
Associates PC

Suyong Bay Landmark Tower

Location: Pusan, Korea
Scheduled for Completion: 2002
Height: 1,516ft (462.1m)
Stories: 102
Area: 2.75 million ft²
Structure: Mixed
Cladding: Glass, aluminum, granite, stainless steel
Use: Multiple

Architect: Kohn Pedersen Fox Associates PC
Structural Engineer: Skilling Ward Magnusson Barkshire
Services Engineer: Ove Arup & Partners
Developer: Daewoo Corporation
Photography: Edge Media courtesy Kohn Pedersen Fox
Associates PC

Table of the 100 Tallest Buildings in the World

The following listing represents data that has been collected by the Council on Tall Buildings and Urban Habitat, on an ongoing basis since the mid 1970s. It features the tallest 100 buildings in the world, at the time of print.
The building's featured in this publication, do not however represent this listing verbatim. Although the efforts of all concerned were enormous, there are a few instances where buildings could not be featured as appropriate material was unfortunately not available. The editors are however absolutely certain that the skyscrapers presented throughout the book are 100 of the tallest, most beautiful and the most significant in the world.

Ranking	BuildingName	City	Completion	Stories	Meters	Feet	Structure	Use
1	Petronas Tower 1	Kuala Lumpur	UC98	88	452.0	1,483	Mixed	Multiple
2	Petronas Tower 2	Kuala Lumpur	UC98	88	452.0	1,483	Mixed	Multiple
3	Sears Tower	Chicago	1974	110	442.0	1,450	Steel	Office
4	Jin Mao Building	Shanghai	UC98	88	420.6	1,380	Mixed	Multiple
5	World Trade Center, One	New York	1972	110	417.0	1,368	Steel	Office
6	World Trade Center, Two	New York	1973	110	415.1	1,362	Steel	Office
7	Empire State Building	New York	1931	102	381.0	1,250	Steel	Office
8	Central Plaza	Hong Kong	1992	78	374.0	1,227	Concrete	Office
9	Bank of China	Hong Kong	1989	70	368.5	1,209	Mixed	Office
10	T & C Tower	Kaoshiung	1997	85	347.5	1,140	Steel	Multiple
11	Amoco Building	Chicago	1973	80	346.3	1,136	Steel	Office
12	John Hancock Center	Chicago	1969	100	343.5	1,127	Steel	Multiple
13	Shun Hing Square	Shenzhen	1996	69	324.9	1,066	Mixed	Office
14	Sky Central Plaza	Guangzhou	1997	80	321.9	1,056	Concrete	Multiple
15	Chicago Beach Tower Hotel	Dubai	UC98	60	321.0	1,053	Mixed	Hotel
16	Baiyoke Tower II	Bangkok	1997	90	320.0	1,050	Concrete	Hotel
17	Chrysler Building	New York	1930	77	318.8	1,046	Steel	Office
18	NationsBank Plaza	Atlanta	1993	55	311.8	1,023	Mixed	Multiple
19	First Interstate World Center	Los Angeles	1990	75	310.3	1,018	Mixed	Office
20	AT&T Corporate Center	Chicago	1989	60	306.9	1,007	Mixed	Office
21	Texas Commerce Tower	Houston	1982	75	304.8	1,000	Mixed	Office
22	Two Prudential Plaza	Chicago	1990	64	303.3	995	Concrete	Office
23	Ryugyong Hotel	Pyongyang	1995	105	299.9	984	Concrete	Hotel
24	Commerzbank Tower	Frankfurt	1997	56	299.0	981	Mixed	Office
25	First Interstate Bank Plaza	Houston	1983	71	296.3	972	Steel	Office
26	Landmark Tower	Yokohama	1993	70	296.3	972	Steel	Multiple
27	311 South Wacker Drive	Chicago	1990	65	292.9	961	Concrete	Office
28	American International Building	New York	1932	67	290.2	952	Steel	Office
29	First Canadian Place	Toronto	1975	72	289.9	951	Steel	Office
30	Society Tower	Cleveland	1991	57	289.6	950	Mixed	Office
31	One Liberty Place	Philadelphia	1987	61	288.0	945	Steel	Office
32	Columbia Seafirst Center	Seattle	1984	76	287.4	943	Mixed	Office
33	40 Wall Street	New York	1930	72	282.6	927	Steel	Office
34	NationsBank Plaza	Dallas	1985	72	280.7	921	Mixed	Office
35	Overseas Union Bank Centre	Singapore	1986	66	280.1	919	Steel	Office
36	United Overseas Bank Plaza	Singapore	1992	66	280.1	919	Steel	Office
37	Republic Plaza	Singapore	1995	66	280.1	919	Mixed	Office
38	Citicorp Center	New York	1977	59	278.9	915	Steel	Multiple
39	Scotia Plaza	Toronto	1989	68	274.9	902	Mixed	Office
40	Transco Tower	Houston	1983	64	274.6	901	Steel	Office
41	Renaissance Tower	Dallas	1975	56	270.1	886	Steel	Office
42	900 North Michigan Avenue	Chicago	1989	66	265.5	871	Mixed	Multiple
43	NationsBank Corporate Center	Charlotte	1992	60	265.5	871	Concrete	Office
44	SunTrust Plaza	Atlanta	1992	60	265.5	871	Concrete	Office
45	Water Tower Place	Chicago	1976	74	261.8	859	Concrete	Multiple
46	First Interstate Tower	Los Angeles	1974	62	262.5	858	Steel	Office
47	Canada Trust Tower	Toronto	1990	51	260.9	856	Mixed	Office
48	Transamerica Corporate Headquarters	San Francisco	1972	48	260.0	853	Mixed	Office
49	G.E. Building	New York	1933	70	259.1	850	Steel	Office
50	One First National Plaza	Chicago	1969	60	259.1	850	Steel	Office

Ranking	Building Name	City	Completion	Stories	Meters	Feet	Structure	Use
51	Two Liberty Place	Philadelphia	1990	58	258.5	848	Steel	Office
52	Messeturm	Frankfurt	1990	63	257.0	843	Concrete	Office
53	USX Tower	Pittsburgh	1970	64	256.3	841	Steel	Office
54	Gate Tower	Osaka	1996	56	253.9	833		Office
55	Osaka World Trade Center	Osaka	1995	55	252.1	827	Steel	Office
56	IBM Tower	Atlanta	1987	50	249.9	820	Mixed	Office
57	BNI City Tower	Jakarta	1995	46	249.9	820	Concrete	Office
58	Korea Life Insurance Company	Seoul	1985	60	249.0	817	Steel	Office
59	CitySpire	New York	1989	75	248.1	814	Concrete	Multiple
60	Rialto Towers	Melbourne	1985	63	248.1	814	Concrete	Office
61	One Chase Manhattan Plaza	New York	1961	60	247.8	813	Steel	Office
62	MetLife Building	New York	1963	59	246.3	808	Steel	Office
63	Shin Kong Life Tower	Taipei	1993	51	244.1	801	Mixed	Office
64	Malayan Bank	Kuala Lumpur	1988	50	243.5	799	Concrete	Office
65	Tokyo City Hall	Tokyo	1991	48	242.9	797	Mixed	Office
66	Woolworth Building	New York	1913	57	241.4	792	Steel	Office
67	Mellon Bank Center	Philadelphia	1991	54	241.4	792	Mixed	Office
68	John Hancock Tower	Boston	1976	60	240.2	788	Steel	Office
69	Bank One Center	Dallas	1987	60	239.9	787	Mixed	Office
70	Commerce Court West	Toronto	1973	57	239.0	784	Mixed	Office
71	Moscow State University	Moscow	1953	26	239.0	784	Steel	Academic
72	Empire Tower	Kuala Lumpur	1994	62	238.1	781	Mixed	Office
73	NationsBank Center	Houston	1984	56	237.7	780	Steel	Office
74	Bank of America Center	San Francisco	1969	52	237.4	779	Steel	Office
75	Worldwide Plaza	New York	1989	47	237.1	778	Steel	Office
76	IDS Center	Minneapolis	1973	52	236.2	775	Mixed	Multiple
77	One Canada Square	London	1991	50	235.9	774	Steel	Office
78	First Bank Place	Minneapolis	1992	58	236.2	775	Mixed	Office
79	Norwest Tower	Minneapolis	1988	57	235.6	773	Steel	Office
80	Treasury Building	Singapore	1986	52	234.7	770	Mixed	Multiple
81	191 Peachtree Tower	Atlanta	1991	50	234.7	770	Mixed	Multiple
82	Opera City Tower	Tokyo	1997	54	234.1	768		Multiple
83	Shinjuku Park Tower	Tokyo	1994	52	232.9	764	Steel	Multiple
84	Heritage Plaza	Houston	1987	52	232.3	762	Steel	Office
85	Kompleks Tun Abdul Razak Building	Penang	1985	65	231.7	760	Concrete	Office
86	Palace of Culture and Science	Warsaw	1955	42	231.0	758	Mixed	Office
87	Carnegie Hall Tower	New York	1991	60	230.7	757	Concrete	Office
88	Three First National Plaza	Chicago	1981	57	229.5	753	Mixed	Office
89	Equitable Tower	New York	1986	51	229.2	752	Steel	Office
90	MLC Centre	Sydney	1978	65	228.9	751	Concrete	Office
91	One Penn Plaza	New York	1972	57	228.6	750	Steel	Office
92	1251 Avenue of the Americas	New York	1972	54	228.6	750	Steel	Office
93	Prudential Tower	Boston	1964	52	228.6	750	Steel	Office
94	Two California Plaza	Los Angeles	1992	52	228.6	750	Steel	Office
95	Gas Company Tower, The	Los Angeles	1991	54	228.3	749	Steel	Office
96	Two Pacific Place/Shangri-La Hotel	Hong Kong	1991	56	228.0	748	Concrete	Multiple
97	1100 Louisiana Building	Houston	1980	55	228.0	748	Mixed	Office
98	Korea World Trade Center	Seoul	1988	54	228.0	748	Steel	Multiple
99	Governor Phillip Tower	Sydney	1993	64	227.1	745	Mixed	Office
100	J.P. Morgan Headquarters	New York	1992	56	227.1	745	Steel	Office

Summary and Fact Sheet

Tallest Building in the World

	Building Name	Location	Height Meters	Feet
to structural top:	Petronas Tower 1 & 2	Kuala Lumpur	452.0	1,483
to highest floor:	Sears Tower	Chicago	436.2	1,431
to top of roof:	Sears Tower	Chicago	442.0	1,450
to tip of spire or antenna:	World Trade Center, One	New York	526.7	1,728

Top 10 Countries, Cities and Regions represented in 100 Tallest List

Country	No. of Buildings	City	No. of Buildings	Region	No. of Buildings
USA	59	New York	18	Africa	0
Japan	6	Chicago	10	Asia	29
Malaysia	5	Houston	6	Europe	4
Canada	4	Los Angeles	4	Mid East	1
Singapore	4	Kuala Lumpur	4	North America	63
Korea	3	Atlanta	4	Oceania	3
China	3	Toronto	4	South America	0
Hong Kong	3	Singapore	4		
Australia	3	Tokyo	3		
Taiwan	2	Philadelphia	3		
Others	8	Others	40		

Total No. of Countries: 18   **Total No. of Cities: 50**

Other Statistics

Date of Construction	No. of Buildings	Material	No. of Buildings	Usage	No. of Buildings
Currently Under Construction:	8	Concrete	18	Academic	1
1990s	34	Mixed	34	Hotel	3
1980s	27	Steel	46	Multiple-Use	19
1970s	17	Not available	2	Office	77
1960s	6			Residential	0
1950s	2				
1940s	0				
1930s	5				
Before 1930	1				

Glossary of Terms

Art Deco
A decorative style stimulated by the Paris Exposition of Modern Decorative and Industrial Arts in 1925, widely used in the architecture of the 1930s, characterized by sharp angular or zig-zag surface forms and ornaments.

Atrium
The main courtyard of a Roman house. Later, a courtyard of a building or a group of buildings. In contemporary architecture, an open multi-floor space within a building.

Caisson
A deep foundation member usually of reinforced concrete used to deliver structural loads to the founding material, installed by excavating.

Campanile
A tall, detached bell tower.

Cantilever
In construction, a portion of a floor or deck extending beyond the vertical column. An overhang.

Colonnade
Row of columns spaced at regular intervals

Cornice
A projecting section of an entablature, also an ornamental molding along the top of a building, wall, or arch, finishing or crowning it.

Cupola
A relatively small dome-like structure on a roof.

Damping
The resistance of a structure to displacement from an externally applied disturbance that is subsequently removed. The resistance may be provided by internal frictional resistance of the elements of the structure, the drag effects of the surrounding medium, or contact with or connection to an adjacent structure.

Finial
The upper portion of a gable, pinnacle, bench-end, or other architectural feature.

Footprint
The space a building takes up at street level.

Framed tube
Perimeter equivalent tube consisting of closely spaced columns and spandrels.

Frieze
A decorative band bearing lettering or sculpture.

Feng Shui
The ancient Chinese art of evaluating buildings to determine how the building will fit within the cosmic balance.

Fenestration
The windows and openings of a building envelope.

Gothic
The architecture of the pointed arch, the rib vault, the flying buttress, the walls reduced to a minimum by spacious arcades, by gallery or triforium, and by spacious clerestory windows. These are not isolated motifs; they act together and represent a system of skeletal structure with active, slender, resilient members and membrane-thin infilling or no infilling at all.

International Style
Architectural style created in the 1920s. Its distinguishing principles are emphasis on volumes, planes, regularity, asymmetry and elegance of materials.

Interstate
A major highway, built as part of the government's national transportation program to connect or join states within the United States.

Mansard roof
A roof with steep sides and a flatter pitch at the top.

Massing
Agglomeration of volume in a building or a region.

Modernism
A style of architecture that came into existence in the 1920s, and had its classical period in the 1930s and the late 1940s.

Moment frame
A building frame system in which lateral shear forces are resisted by shear and flexure in members and joints of the frame.

Moment-resisting frame
An integrated system of structural elements possessing continuity and hence capable of resisting bending forces.

Mullions
The horizontal or vertical members of a window wall or curtain wall system that are normally attached to the floor slab or beams, and support the glass and/or elements of a window wall.

Pilaster
An engaged column, a shallow pier or an architectural element projecting from a wall.

Post-Modernism
In architecture, a break with the canons of International Style Modernism. Functionalism and emphasis on the expression of structure are rejected in favor of a greater freedom of design. There is a new interplay of contemporary forms and materials, with frequent historical allusions, often ironic. Post-Modernism also accepts the manifestations of commercial mass culture—bright colors, neon lights, and advertising signs.

Rebar
Steel reinforcing bars used in concrete structures.

Reveal
The side of an opening for a door or window, doorway, or the like, between the door-frame or window frame and the outer surface of the wall; where the opening is not filled with the door or window, the whole thickness of the wall.

Setback
The withdrawal of the face of a building to a line some distance from the boundary of the property or from the street or from a lower segment of the building.

Slip form
A form which moves in stages during placing of concrete. Movement may be either horizontal or vertical.

Spandrel
That part of a wall between the head of a window and the sill of the window above it. (An upturned spandrel continues above the roof or floor line.)

Spandrel beam
Floor level beams in the faces of a building, usually supporting the edges of the floor slabs.

Terrazzo
A mosaic flooring composed of chips of marble and cement.

Tripartite
Division of a tall building into three parts: base, shaft and capital.

Tube-in-tube system
A building with an inner core tube system and an exterior perimeter tube system.

Truss
A structure built up of members designed primarily to resist tension or compression.

Wainscoting
A paneling of solid wood for an interior wall, especially the lower part.

Council on Tall Buildings and Urban Habitat

SPONSORING SOCIETIES

International Association for Bridge and Structural Engineering (IABSE)
American Society of Civil Engineers (ASCE)
American Institute of Architects (AIA)
American Planning Association (APA)
International Union of Architects (UIA)
American Society of Interior Designers (ASID)
Japan Structural Consultants Association (JSCA)
Urban Land Institute (ULI)
International Federation of Interior Designers (IFI)

AFFILIATED ORGANIZATIONS

Australian Council on Tall Buildings and Urban Habitat
Council on Tall Buildings and Urban Habitat—Grupo Brasil
Centre for Asian Tall Buildings and Urban Habitat
Chicago Committee on High-Rise Buildings
Dutch Council on Tall Buildings
Los Angeles Tall Buildings Structural Design Council
Polish Group on Tall Buildings and Urban Habitat

ORGANIZATIONAL MEMBERS

PATRONS

Carrier Corporation, Farmington
Consolidated Contractors International Company, Athens
Zuhair Fayez Partnership, Jeddah
T.R. Hamzah & Yeang Sdn Bhd, Selangor
Kuala Lumpur City Centre (Holdings) Sdn Bhd, Kuala Lumpur
Kuwait Foundation for the Advancement of Sciences (KFAS), Kuwait
Otis Elevator Co., Farmington
Ranhill Bersekutu Sdn Bhd, Kuala Lumpur

SPONSORS

Al Rayes Group, Kuwait
EUROPROFIL Strategie, Luxembourg
HL-Technik AG, Munich
Hochtief, Essen
Hongkong Land Ltd, Hong Kong
Jaros, Baum & Bolles, New York
Kajima Corporation, Tokyo
John A. Martin & Associates, Inc., Los Angeles
Walter P. Moore & Associates, Inc., Houston
Multiplex Constructions (NSW) Pty Ltd, Sydney
Nippon Steel, Tokyo
Ove Arup Partnership, London
Permasteelisa SPA, San Vendemiano
Leslie E. Robertson Associates, R.L.L.P., New York
Samsung Engineering & Construction Co., Ltd, Seoul
Saudi Consulting Services, Riyadh
Schindler Elevator Corporation, Randolph
Skidmore, Owings & Merrill, LLP, Chicago
Syska & Hennessy, New York
Takenaka Corporation, Tokyo
Thornton-Tomasetti/Engineers, New York
Tishman Speyer Properties, New York
WARCENT S.A., Warsaw
Wing Tai Construction & Engineering Co., Hong Kong
Wong & Ouyang (HK) Ltd, Hong Kong

DONORS

American Iron and Steel Institute, Washington DC
Lynn S. Beedle, Hellertown
China Jingye Construction Engineering, Beijing
Hart Consultant Group, Santa Monica
Hollandsche Beton Maatschappij B.V., Rijswijk
Hong Kong Housing Authority, Hong Kong
The Kling-Lindquist Partnership, Inc., Philadelphia
Kohn Pedersen Fox Associates PC, New York
Kone Elevators, Brussels
Leigh & Orange Ltd, Hong Kong
Mueser Rutledge Consulting Engineers, New York
Norman Disney & Young, Brisbane
Pei Cobb Freed & Partners, New York
Projest Consultoria e Projetos S.C. Ltd, Rio de Janeiro
Shenzhen University, Institute of Architectural Design and
    Research, Shenzhen
Skilling Ward Magnusson Barkshire Inc., Seattle
Nabih Youssef and Associates, Los Angeles

CONTRIBUTORS

American Institute of Steel Construction, Chicago
PT Arnan Pratama Consultants, Jakarta
Aronsohn Raadegevende Ing., Rotterdam
Boundary Layer Wind Tunnel Laboratory (U. Western Ontario),
    London
Bovis Construction Group, London
Crone Associates Pty Ltd, Sydney
Institute Sultan Iskandar, Johor
INTEMAC, Madrid
Land Development Corporation, Hong Kong
Lim Consultants Inc., Cambridge
Meinhardt Australia Pty Ltd, Melbourne
Meinhardt Consulting Engineers., Hong Kong
Metodo Engenharia S/A, Sao Paulo
Middlebrook & Louie, San Francisco
Mitchell McFarlane Brentnall & Partners Int'l Ltd, Hong Kong
Mori Building Company Ltd, Tokyo
Charles Pankow Builders, Inc., Altadena
John Portman & Associates, Inc., Atlanta
PSM International, Chicago
Rahulan Zain Associates, Kuala Lumpur
Schwimann Consultants, Paris
Siecor Corporation, Hickory
Teng & Associates, Inc., Chicago
The Turner Corporation, New York
Wan Hin & Company Ltd, Hong Kong
Wong Hobach Lau Consulting Engineers, Los Angeles

Council on Tall Buildings and Urban Habitat continued

CONTRIBUTING PARTICIPANTS

ACTEC Consulting Engineers, Bangkok
ADK Consulting Engineers, Athens
Allen Allen & Hemsley, Brisbane
Anglo American Property Services (Pty) Ltd, Johannesburg
Architectural Services Dept, Hong Kong
Australian Institute of Steel Construction, Milsons Point
Bonacci Winward Consulting Structural Civil Engineers, Melbourne
Brandow & Johnston Associates, Los Angeles
Brooke Hillier Parker, Hong Kong
Buildings & Data S.A., Brussels
Buro Happold, Bath
Callison Architecture, Inc., Seattle
CBM Engineers, Inc., Houston
Cermak Peterka Petersen, Inc., Fort Collins
CMA Architects & Engineers, San Juan
CMPS & F Pty Ltd, Sydney
Connell Wagner Pty Ltd, South Melbourne
Constructora Menezes Cortes, Ltda, Rio de Janeiro
Crane Fulview Door Co., Lake Bluff
Davis Langdon & Everest, London
DeSimone, Chaplin & Dobryn, Inc., New York
DeStefano & Partners, Chicago
Drahtseilerei Kocks, Mulheim
ECT Consulting Engineers, Quezon City
Edgett Williams Consulting Group, Mill Valley
Flack & Kurtz Consulting Engineers, New York
Sir Norman Foster and Partners, London
Halpern Glick Maunsell, Leederville
Hellmuth, Obata & Kassabaum, Inc., San Francisco
HLW International LLP, New York
Iffland Kavanagh Waterbury, PC, New York
IGH Ing. Ges. Hoepfner mbH, Cologne
Ing. Muller Marl GmbH, Marl
International Iron & Steel Institute, Brussels
Raul J. Izquierdo Ingeniero Civil, Mexico

Jeon and Associates, Seoul
J. A. Jones Construction Co., Charlotte
Lerch, Bates & Associates Ltd, Littleton
Stanley D. Lindsey & Associates, Nashville
Joseph R. Loring & Associates, Inc, New York
Low & Hooke (AUST) Pty Ltd, Leichhardt
LPC Arquitetura Ltda, Rio de Janeiro
Marcq & Roba, Brussels
Martin & Huang International Inc., Pasadena
Enrique Martinez-Romero, S.A., Mexico
Maunsell Consultants (Singapore) Pte Ltd, Singapore
Mitsubishi Estate Co., Ltd, Tokyo
MPN Group Pty Ltd, Milsons Point
NBBJ, Seattle
Nikken Sekkei Ltd, Tokyo
Nishikian & Associates, San Francisco
N V Besix S.A., Brussels
Obayashi Corporation, Tokyo
Omrania & Associates, Riyadh
Ove Arup & Partners, Melbourne
Park Tower Group, New York
Cesar Pelli & Associates, Inc., New Haven
Quantum Field Sdn Bhd, Kuala Lumpur
RFB Consulting Architects, Johannesburg
Rocco Design Limited, Hong Kong
Rowan Williams Davies & Irwin Inc., Guelph
Samwoo Architects & Engineers, Seoul
Samyn and Partners, Brussels
Sato & Boppana, Los Angeles
SJPH Design Partnership, North Sydney
SOBRENCO, S.A., Rio de Janeiro
Southern African Institute of Steel Construction, Johannesburg
Steel Reinforcement Institute of Australia, Sydney
Chris P. Stefanos Associates Inc., Oak Lawn
STS Consultants, Ltd, Deerfield
Taylor Thomson Whitting Pty Ltd, St. Leonards
Tooley & Company, Los Angeles
Tractebel Development S.A., Brussels
United States Gypsum Co., Chicago
University of Nebraska, College of Architecture, Lincoln
B.A. Vavaroutas & Associates, Ltd, Athens
Villa Real Ltd/SA, Brussels
Wind Engineering Institute Co. Ltd, Tokyo
Wisma SSP, Selangor
CC Wong Consulting Engineers, Kuala Lumpur
Yolles Group Inc., Canada

Index

Denotes buildings under construction

An Acknowledgment

When, at the initiative of the Council on Tall Buildings and Urban Habitat (CTBUH), I first undertook to prepare *100 of the World's Tallest Buildings* 10 years ago, there was a list of 100, occasionally updated and published by the Council. Along with that list, which kept changing as new and ever taller buildings were added to it (and those at the bottom dropped out) there was also a 'Glossary' of technical terms selected by the Council in order to make the descriptive texts more accessible; it defined the occasional technical, structural or architectural term not always familiar to interested readers. CTBUH also devised the criteria for ranking the buildings and arriving at precise measurements for their height (that is: sidewalk at the main entrance to the structural top of the building, but no TV or radio antennas or flag poles are to be included).

As I approached the task, there were one hundred plus buildings to verify, discover, and describe. Often it meant travelling to their locations, photographing them, and obtaining from varied sources their plans, sections, elevations, details and photographs. For some more obscure ones, this meant researching the library materials during their construction earlier in this century, for their architects, and engineers had passed away long ago and ownership changed so frequently that it sometimes required the approach of a detective to reach closure. Large numbers of these buildings can be found in the two major homes of the early skyscraper, New York City and Chicago, but as the book illustrates, today they are to be found on five continents: North America, Europe, Africa, Asia and Australia.

In the process of compiling information from the early stages of a building's conception and initial news releases, there were buildings planned to surpass the tallest and claim future championship that were never built (for example, Trump City's proposed 150 story, 1,670-foot-tall building, and the skyneedle in Chicago which was to rise 400 feet higher than the Sears Tower). Then there were buildings under construction that, instead of being completed, were suspended, never finished, or even slated for demolition. The most elusive category of buildings are those that changed ownership and thus their names—occasionally several times in succession, for example 40 Wall Street (Bank of Manhattan Building) which is now the Trump Building and Rockefeller Center's centerpiece, the R.C.A. Building, which is now G.E., just as the world-famous Pan-Am is now MetLife.

Over the years, several generations of students at Lehigh helped at earlier or later stages of the research. I would like to thank the following: Jared Dellavalle, Dariush Derakshani, Sharon Khosla, Lisa Gilman, Eric Lewis, Daniel Levine, Jill Lipovski, James Lynch, Colin Smith, Linda Stone, Karen Wagner and Peter Zuraw.

Matthew Smith of Casaccio Architects, Havertown, Pennsylvania, started work on the project as a student and continued beyond graduation by taking increasingly more interest and responsibility. He well deserves not only a special mention, but a sharing of the credits.

In order to bring this book to publication many have helped; this list cannot be sufficiently exhaustive to mention every architect or engineer, real estate office or building owner, who have helped by sharing information with us. We thank them all. A special gratitude is due to Douglas Mason, photographer, who lent his expertise to 'plug the gaps' in our pictorial account of several crucial buildings.

Finally I am deeply indebted to the Graham Foundation for Advanced Studies in the Fine Arts for their grant which has helped defray the cost of research, travel and photography as well as clerical assistance over the years.

Ivan Zaknic
Lehigh University